Real World Testimonials About
The 6 Types of Working Genius

"Nothing gave me an 'aha' moment like the Working Genius. It dialed in something for me that's been a question for years. It gave me a sense of freedom."

—Michael Hyatt, *New York Times* best-selling author

"The simple ten-minute assessment completely changed the way we think about our work and our people."

—Andrew Laffoon, CEO, Mixbook

"I can't tell you all enough how 'less crazy' this model makes me feel. It really is a game-changer in getting work done—and done well."

—Stephanie Culbreth, business execution consultant

"If helping your people find fulfillment in their work is important for you, apply Lencioni's Working Genius in your organization."

—Bobby Herrera, president, Populus Group

"Working Genius has helped me realize the geniuses that I never knew I had, and now I am able to intentionally spend time doing the things I love. It's brought so much fulfillment to my life and work!"

—Stacy Rutten, professional development coach,
Buffalo-Hanover-Montrose School District

"Understanding my working geniuses, competencies, and frustrations told me more about myself than the other personality profiles I have done. And in more than twenty years in the classroom, using the Working Genius model resulted in the most productive project I have ever organized."

—Al Ainsworth, tenth grade teacher, Northpoint Christian School

"What a powerful tool for understanding the contributions each individual can bring to a team."

—Selita Jansen, operations leadership, TrueNorth Companies

"In this compelling book, Pat Lencioni shows us how work flows easily when we unleash our inner genius."

—Steve Strauss, columnist, *USA Today*

"The Working Genius has reframed our entire perception of our effectiveness as a team."

—Mark Stuckey, assistant high school principal, Solanco School District

"Working Genius has transformed my interaction with volunteers. It has offered insight to them that adds value to their lives, but also helps us with engagement. I am striving to never place a volunteer in an area outside of their geniuses."

—Carmen Halsey, director of leadership development,
Illinois Baptist State Association

"With his usual elegance, Lencioni provides a straightforward tool to help us understand and engage team members. *The 6 Types of Working Genius* will empower every manager to affect positive change for their people, and be responsible for improving their productivity, both personally as well as professionally."

—Sam Weinstein, CEO, SpecialtyCare, Inc.

"*The Five Dysfunctions of a Team* is the book that helped Thirty Tigers shape its culture like no other. I enjoyed *The 6 Types of Working Genius* immensely, and my mind is racing with how I can incorporate the insights gleaned from it into my company's operations."

—David Macias, cofounder and president, Thirty Tigers

"This transformative book aligns perfectly with our evolving understanding of leadership, that the best teams and organizations have leaders who intentionally discover, honor, and leverage the strengths—or Genius—of their team members. I can't wait to use this simple and actionable framework with my team."

—Jennifer McCollum, CEO, Linkage, Inc.

"After many years in marriage and business together, I questioned if my wife hated all my ideas. Before the Working Genius, I saw her discernment as conflict instead of complement. Taking the assessment was the best anniversary gift!"

—Heath Ellenberger, operational partner, OrangeTheory Fitness

"I've lived under constant pressure to always be creative and inventive. I've felt judged for not being good in those areas. It's such a relief to finally understand that these are not my gifts and that I have other geniuses I can leverage."

—Kevin Tranel, campus pastor, The Chapel

"Your life will be transformed by aligning your work to your genius."

—Ellen Twomey, founder, You are techY

"This is the simplest and most useful tool that I have come across to quickly improve personal and team energy, understanding, and productivity."

—Bates Alheit, senior consultant, Convergenc3

"Patrick Lencioni does it again! In *The 6 Types of Working Genius,* he uses the power of story to draw in the reader, then issues an important call to action. He challenges leaders to help their people unpack their innate talents and leverage them, not just for the benefit of the organization, but for the direct benefits they can reap by living a more fulfilled life."

—Kelly Goldsmith, PhD, professor of marketing, Vanderbilt University

"I love living into who God has made me to be."

—Scott Langhans, associate pastor, Mission Church

Also by Patrick Lencioni

THE 6 TYPES OF WORKING GENIUS

A Better Way to Understand Your Gifts, Your Frustrations, and Your Team

PATRICK LENCIONI

Matt Holt Books
An Imprint of BenBella Books, Inc.
Dallas, TX

Matt Holt is an imprint of BenBella Books, Inc.
10440 N. Central Expressway
Suite 800
Dallas, TX 75231
benbellabooks.com
Send feedback to feedback@benbellabooks.com

BenBella and *Matt Holt* are federally registered trademarks.

Printed in the United States of America
10 9 8 7 6 5 4 3 2 1

Library of Congress Control Number: 2022937041
ISBN 9781637743294 (hardcover)
ISBN 9781637743300 (electronic)

Copyediting by Michael Fedison
Proofreading by Lisa Story and Cape Cod Compositors, Inc.
Text design and composition by Jordan Koluch
Cover design by Grant Willingham
Printed by Lake Book Manufacturing

Special discounts for bulk sales are available.
Please contact bulkorders@benbellabooks.com.

This book is dedicated to my son Matthew. Without your insights, this project could not have happened, and it would not have been so darn much fun for me.

Contents

INTRODUCTION

This book is based on two undeniable truths.

First, people who utilize their natural, God-given talents are much more fulfilled and successful than those who don't.

Second, teams and organizations that help people tap into their God-given talents are much more successful and productive than those that don't.

As obvious as all this may be, the reality remains that most people aren't terribly fulfilled in their work, which makes sense because most people don't really understand their work-related gifts. As a result, most teams don't come anywhere close to tapping into their members' talents and achieving their true potential. The question that has to be asked is, why haven't we solved this problem yet?

It's certainly not because we haven't tried. There are several wonderful tools out there that help us better understand our personalities and our preferences. I've been using many of them for years. The problem has always been trying to figure out how they translate to the day-to-day experience of doing real work, of every kind, and with teammates who have different gifts.

I am happy to be able to say that *The Six Types of Working Genius* solves that very problem! Not only does it provide a framework for quickly understanding your unique talents, it does so within the context of a new model for how any type of work gets done. In other words, it's as much a productivity tool as it is a personality model.

I have to admit that I didn't sit down one day to try to solve this problem; it came about largely by accident. I was simply struggling with my own fluctuations between joy and exasperation at work, and someone (thank you, Amy!) asked me the big question: Why are you like this? It wasn't an accusation or a judgment, but a real question asked out of curiosity and a desire to help me figure out why I was too frequently frustrated working in my own company, with good friends, in a field that I thoroughly enjoyed. I had no idea that answering that question would provoke the advent of the model that I present in this book. And I certainly didn't know that it would lead to an assessment that has already proven more practical and immediately helpful in changing people's lives—including my own—than anything we've ever done at The Table Group. From finding more joy in their jobs, to having a better understanding of their spouse or children, to reorganizing their teams to better align with team members' geniuses, we have been gladly overwhelmed by the stories sent to us by people who have found immediate and lasting relief through the Working Genius Model and Assessment.

Like most of my books, the first part is a fable that provides a fictional—but realistic—story around Working Genius and its application. The second part is a thorough overview of the model itself. I pray that *The Six Types of Working Genius* will allow you, and those you work with, to become the people God created you to be, and that your team, organization, and even family will benefit as a result.

THE FABLE

JOB

Work isn't life. But it's a big part of it. And though I wish it weren't true, for years it had a more frustrating impact on mine than I wanted or expected. Thankfully, I recently figured some things out that made that impact much more positive, and just in the nick of time, because my life was about to unravel.

I'm Bull Brooks, by the way. I know that sounds like I should be a musician, either country or rap depending on how you look at it. My real name is Jeremiah, but somehow because of that '70s song about the frog, people started calling me Bull when I was a kid, and it stuck. Everyone but my kids calls me Bull. I suppose one day even they might use that moniker, but for now, it's still "Dad."

My full name is actually Jeremiah Octavian Brooks, which is a handful, or a mouthful. St. Octavian was a martyr back in the fifth century, and for some reason that I don't recall her telling me, my mom must have liked him. One of the interesting things about all this is that my initials are JOB. I suppose that I

shouldn't be surprised that I've developed something of an obses-
sion with work.

But enough about me and my crazy name. Let me tell you
about how work almost ruined me, and what I learned that
changed everything.

WORK

I should probably start by explaining my earliest understanding of work, which came from my parents.

What I remember most about my dad's job is that he didn't seem to choose it freely. I mean, without a college education and living in a relatively unsophisticated town, there weren't a ton of options. Being an insurance adjuster—I have to admit that I didn't completely understand what that meant until I got into my first car accident—isn't the most fascinating job in the world, but it's not the worst one either. He had time for the family and spent at least half his time indoors.

As for my mom, she ran our household and organized most of what happened there. She seemed to like almost every aspect of her work, whether it was teaching us to read, volunteering at school, or paying the bills. Other than the laundry, which she wisely and effectively delegated to us, she never complained about her daily work, and often declared that every day with us was a joy. I think she honestly meant it.

But whether my dad liked his job or not, I can't say. It wasn't really a topic of conversation, or perhaps, consideration. Other than the time he said, "Bull, if it was fun, they wouldn't call it work," it didn't really cross my mind whether he found his job fulfilling or not. For my dad, work was something you did to pay the mortgage and tuition at St. Catherine of Siena School. Enough said.

It was only after having my own first job working as a bank teller that I decided my dad's approach to labor would not be my own.

LAWN MOWING

Speaking of my dad, he was a great guy. In the fifties, people would have called him "swell," though I'm not sure why I need to tell you that. He was affable and responsible and frugal. Swell.

One of his favorite activities was the Saturday morning ritual of mowing the lawn. Of course, it wasn't just mowing. That was the fun part, and it was reserved mostly for Dad. It also involved raking leaves, picking up leaves, pulling weeds, hoeing weeds, sweeping things, and picking up things, followed by the grand finale of spraying off the driveway and sidewalk with the power hose.

Because I obeyed my dad, I pulled myself out of bed and went outside every Saturday when what I really wanted to be doing was watching cartoons or Major League Baseball on TV. But I helped him mow the lawn. And I hated it. I never really understood why, and it bothered me because I loved my dad. But it was torture.

Well, a few months ago, I finally discovered where my frustration with the Saturday morning ritual came from, which is the subject of my story here. I wish I could have explained it to my dad way back then, and certainly before he died. It would have avoided some unnecessary frustration between us, and I might just have been able to watch more cartoons and ball games.

Sorry about that, Dad.

JOY

Though I didn't get my first real job at the bank until my senior year in high school, I did a variety of odd things here and there to make money during my teen years.

One summer, I went out near the oil fields and performed the exciting work of propping up metal targets shaped like animals at a shooting range. Diving into a foxhole and listening to bullets fly over my head was probably the greatest motivation I ever had for going to college.

I also remember another summer when I helped my next-door neighbor who had a side business insulating attics. My job entailed standing in the back of an enclosed metal truck in 110-degree weather, making sure that I didn't lose a finger while spreading out fiberglass gook into what I can only describe as an insulation chipper. It's a wonder I didn't go all the way for a PhD.

Then came my bank job. (Wow, that kind of sounds like I robbed the place.)

Now, I'm sure some people are cut out to be bank tellers, and I'm equally sure that I'm not one of them. No matter how hard

I tried, my register would always be out of balance at the end of the day. I could never understand why that was such a big deal.

Sometimes I'd be off by just a few pennies or a couple of dollars, and I'd offer to pay the difference out of my own pocket. The manager would say, "That's not how it works," and we'd spend the next hour or so trying to figure out where I hit the wrong button on the cash register thing.

I think they kept me on at the bank because the ladies—all of the tellers were women—liked having me around. I made them, and the customers, laugh a lot. Which probably explains why I was out of balance half the time, too. I especially liked it when I got to work at the drive-thru window, the one with the pneumatic tube that swooshed people their money in a canister to the outside lane. I'd often send customers a bottle of ketchup or something else from the refrigerator just to make them laugh.

What I remember most from that job, though, is the woman who worked the teller station next to me. Her name was Joy, and she was so darned nice. She was married, had a couple of children, and was not someone that a seventeen-year-old boy would expect to call a friend. But she laughed at my jokes, helped me when I didn't understand the difference between a cashier's check and a money order, and took an interest in me as a person. I grew quite fond of her.

By the end of the summer, I remember being amazed at how much I respected and enjoyed being around Joy, and I won't forget what she told me.

"Bull, don't be like me. Find something you like doing so it won't feel like work." I tried to assure her that her job wasn't so bad. She just waved off my remark and said, "Don't settle, my little friend."

Those words came back to haunt me just a few years later.

COLLEGE CONFUSION

In college, I did a little less than my fair share of partying. Growing up poor-ish (I have nothing to complain about) I felt a duty to my parents, who were paying most of my tuition, to take school seriously. And so, I worked hard.

Unfortunately, I had little guidance when it came time to choose a major.

I settled on economics because it seemed like a good mix of practicality and liberal arts. What I mean is that it was neither a blow-off major (I don't want to offend anyone who studied interpretative dance, but . . .) nor a technical grind (electrical engineering with an emphasis on mathematics cannot be fun for anyone, can it?). You know what I mean.

By the time I graduated, I wasn't sure what I had learned about economics. To this day, I can tell you about something called the supply and demand curves, and that's about it. I wish I were joking.

When it came time to get a job, I was pretty lost, so I used a sophisticated approach: find out which companies were hiring and paying well. And I'm ashamed to admit this. I really am. But I took a job in banking.

Okay, I wasn't a teller, but still. I was doing financial analysis of something or other—I can't even say the rest of it. I think I've blocked it out of my brain. And I hated it. The people who hired me said I would like it and be successful. After all, I was an economics major, and somehow I graduated toward the top of my class. And the job was not just with a bank; it was with an *investment* bank. It paid quite well. The office was impressive. My friends were jealous of me.

But I was miserable.

For almost two years, which was the longest decade of my life, I tried to be successful. I tapped into all of my discipline and intellectual muscle to try and overcome my lack of interest and convince myself that this job was my ticket to a successful career. But it took its toll on me, physically and emotionally. Just as I was about to decide to abandon my hope that I would ever make it in investment banking, my boss did the merciful work of abandoning it for me. I was like a horse with a broken leg, and I was relieved to be put out of my misery.

But I was also lost.

FALSE REBOUND

Dusting off my pride and my resume, I decided to be a little more discerning in my search for a new job. And you will not believe what I'm about to tell you. I went to work for another bank.

Now, before you write me off as a lunatic or a glutton for punishment, understand that I was not actually doing banking. I got a job in marketing.

I can't tell you how much of a relief it was to be out of the nuts and bolts of banking. And I was quite confident that marketing would be better. Unfortunately, my new role turned out to be almost as much of a grind as my last one.

Within the year, I found myself constantly complaining to my girlfriend, Anna—who would later become my wife—about how much my job was driving me crazy. Though Anna was and continues to be a patient woman, I could tell that she was starting to get a little tired of hearing about my work woes. "You really need to find something you enjoy," she'd exhort me again and again.

Anna was working for a firm that organized events for client companies. To be honest, it was really hard work, forcing her to be on the road for as much as half the year. And while the travel itself grew wearisome for her, Anna seemed to like her job. She certainly didn't complain about it. And more importantly, she didn't get the Sunday Blues.

SUNDAY BLUES

You probably know what I'm talking about—those feelings you get during halftime of the Sunday night football game, or whatever else you're doing on Sunday night, when you realize that you are just twelve hours from having to go back to work. I had them when I worked at the investment bank, and I had them in my marketing job.

And if that weren't bad enough, I started getting them earlier and earlier on weekends. Sometimes I'd be out with Anna on a date on *Saturday* night, and I would start feeling a sense of dread that I couldn't put my finger on. And then it would dawn on me. The job.

Now, you might be wondering whether I had just chosen particularly bad companies to work for. I wondered the same thing myself. But looking back, I must admit that those first two firms, and the handful of managers I had in each of them, were a little above average. The people I worked for took a greater interest in me than I could have expected, and they really liked their work. And they wanted me to like it, too.

It's just that I didn't. And I was starting to panic.

DESPERATE

At that point I was willing to try anything to stop dreading work, so I talked to the handful of people I knew who actually liked their jobs. I met with a happy lawyer and decided he was deranged. Just kidding. I talked to a management consultant, a teacher, and a computer programmer.

When I asked them what they liked about their jobs, their answers made no sense to me. They talked vaguely about law, business, education, and technology, but their answers weren't all that compelling. I was starting to think that there was just something wrong with me, and that I was destined for a lifetime of misery at work. Heck, I even met an insurance adjuster when I wrecked my car, and he seemed to like his work just fine, though he couldn't really tell me why.

I felt no closer to discovering the key to an enjoyable job, and I don't say this lightly. I was starting to slide into a mild depression. And anyone who knows anything about depression understands that even a mild case is awful. And then, thanks be to God, one day at work we had a meeting with an advertising agency.

We were doing a campaign around a new 401(k) offering, or something equally boring to me, and we did a focus group with a bunch of people in their thirties about how they envisioned our company's brand. The facilitators would ask people questions like, "If AFS [I worked for a company called Accelerated Financial Systems] were a person who walked into the room right now, what would he or she look like?" Yeah, it sounds ridiculous, but there was something about it that I found interesting.

Anyway, after the focus group ended, I asked a woman from the advertising agency about her firm. She told me that the company was growing and that they were looking for people.

So, I re-dusted off my resume, sent it to her and some guy in human resources, and several weeks later, I was gladly telling people at cocktail parties that I worked in advertising. I promise I'm not that shallow. It was just fun to say, "I work in advertising."

But here's the best part. The Sunday Blues went away.

BLISSFUL IGNORANCE

Even though I was twenty-six years old, I had to start at the bottom rung of the agency. Which meant I was assigned the smallest clients. One of my first jobs was doing a campaign for—get this—a petting zoo. I kid you not.

One of the partners at our firm had a friend who had a cousin whose wife played golf with a woman who owned a friggin' petting zoo. And he, the partner, agreed to help her with advertising for almost nothing. Which means they went in search of the least experienced, lowest-paid people in the firm. That was me and a guy named Jasper Jones. Yes, Jasper Jones. I had never known another person with that first name. He made it clear that he was Jasper, and not Casper, of the friendly ghost variety, and prohibited me from ever calling him that. So, when I really, really wanted to tease him, I called him Casper.

Anyway, Jasper and I were assigned the task of helping a petting zoo attract more "petters." As ridiculous as that sounds, I had to admit that I loved that work more than any I'd ever done.

We researched all the elementary schools and preschools and

youth groups and Boys & Girls Clubs in the area and talked to a dozen principals and teachers and administrators. We designed everything from flyers to T-shirts to buttons—yes, buttons—to give away at the zoo. To be fair, I did most of the design parts, and Jasper made sure we pulled it all together.

He and I were teased mercilessly by our colleagues, who referred to our work as the Llama Project. And though I had to pretend it was a silly assignment, I wasn't complaining.

For the better part of a year, we did all kinds of other lower-level client work at the firm. Most of the time, we were arranging newspaper ads or hiring people to hand out leaflets on the street or helping clients design coffee mugs and signage for their small businesses.

But somehow, I didn't mind. And I didn't know why. And I didn't care. I was happier. Anna was happier. Jasper was happy. Who cares what the reason was?

A few years later, I realized that I should have cared.

MONTAGE

For the next two or three years, my life was mostly free of work drudgery and dread. What a relief!

I began to get better clients, make a little more money, and climb the proverbial corporate ladder. Oddly enough, there was actually a ladder in the office that people used to get books that were high on the shelves in our library.

During that time, Anna and I got married and had our first little boy, whom we named Heifer. She thought it was cute that he and his father had names that sounded like cattle.

Of course, we did no such thing. He was Matthew, and his middle name was Octavian, which meant his acronym was MOB. Anna barely let me use my middle name, but I convinced her that it wouldn't mean little Matthew would grow up to become a member of a gang or the mafia.

Anyway, life was rolling, and I didn't even remember what the Sunday Blues felt like.

And then something terrible happened.

I was promoted.

CONGRATULATIONS ON YOUR LOSS

That's right. More money. A real office. More responsibility. I was ecstatic.

For about a month.

Slowly, and almost imperceptibly, my joy at work began to fade.

At some point, every day became just a little less satisfying. An issue here. A conversation there. A difficult client over there. I found myself having just the slightest twinge of dread while watching a movie with Anna one Sunday evening. What was happening?

Of course, I didn't dare mention anything to her. Now that she was working part-time and we were trying to have another baby, Anna needed me to be stable in my job. And so, I wrote it off as a temporary, minor hiccup, a small bump on my never-ending road toward vocational Oz.

And then came the annual performance review cycle. I had only been in the new role for two months, so I wasn't even sure

I would have to go through the process. But I did, and it wasn't pretty.

Okay, it wasn't exactly a train wreck. But almost every area where I was evaluated had earned me a "meets expectations" grade, with a few falling in the "needs some work to meet expectations" category. Still, I was pissed. I mean, I had never gotten anything lower than a B- in any class in school. And as bad as I was in banking and finance, I actually loved advertising. This was a serious dip in the upward slope of my career graph.

My manager, Chaz Westerfield III (and yes, his name was perfectly suited to his personality), said that my "unspectacular" review was probably just because I was new, and that he "would rather be hard on me and have me improve than go easy and allow me to fade."

"I'm not going to fade, Chaz. This is just a surprise."

He tried half-heartedly to console me. "Well, you're generally meeting expectations."

"Come on, man. That's a pretty low bar. I just don't see where the problem is. My clients are happy."

"Are you happy?"

I responded reflexively. "Yeah, I'm happy. I mean, do I seem like I'm not happy? I'm doing—"

Chaz interrupted, shaking his head. "Bull, you don't seem happy." He paused as I digested his surprising comments. "And your people don't seem all that happy."

I started to get defensive. "They don't seem all that happy? What does that even mean? How does someone even know—"

He interrupted again. "I asked them."

I was frozen. What could I say?

Years later, I would learn from one of my employees who would eventually work with me again that Chaz had misrepresented my team's feedback, and that they had told him they were concerned about *my* unhappiness, not theirs. But I didn't know that; I just assumed I was out of touch and that he was telling the truth. Regardless, I wasn't feeling warm toward Chaz at that moment.

"Well, Chaz. What kind of name is that, by the way? I mean, it fits you because you're a pompous ass, and you were probably given a trust fund and a Range Rover when you were sixteen."

I'm so glad I didn't actually say that. I wanted to, but even in my confused and defensive state, I knew it wasn't true or fair. I mean, he probably did get a Range Rover when he turned sixteen, and he would definitely justify the use of the term *pompous*, but who was I to judge him? This wasn't all Chaz's fault—as far as I knew at the time—even if I didn't like the guy.

"Listen, Chaz. What you're saying is right, and this is my challenge. And, darn it, I'm going to take responsibility for myself and my team and use this disappointing review to motivate me to get better."

I didn't say that, either. I wish I had, but I didn't. I just sat there frowning and wondering what I was going to tell Anna.

We wrapped up the review, and true to the hardheaded nature of my name, I went back to my office and decided to handle this quietly, and on my own. So, for the next six months, I grinded. And spent less time at home. And when I was home, I was kind of grumpy. Hell, I was pretty grumpy at work, too.

Anna was swamped and stressed with Matthew—oh, after he got over his colicky stage, we learned he had a peanut allergy—and less than patient with my new attitude. And though I won't go into the details here, it was causing problems. Or I should say, *I* was causing problems.

I wasn't as attentive as I should have been to Anna's challenges at home. I was often short with her. I even started complaining about having to change Matthew's diaper, though my share of that dirty work couldn't have been more than 3 or 4 percent. The truth was, I was behaving neither rationally nor patiently. Though Anna could see it more clearly than I could, I was certainly not proud of myself.

A few months later, Anna and I finally had the big conversation. We were in the kitchen having In-N-Out Burgers and cream soda for dinner while Matthew was asleep. It went like this . . .

> **Bull**: "I don't want to tell you this, but I'm hating my job again."
>
> **Anna** (confused and crying): "What? Not again."
>
> **Me** (panicking): "Don't worry. It's not that bad. I'll figure something out."
>
> **Anna** (still crying, but not really upset): "I know you will. By the way, I'm pregnant."
>
> **Me** (shocked): "What? I mean, fantastic! Don't worry about my job. I'll figure something out."

At that moment, most of my thoughts about work disappeared, and we just celebrated.

Two hours later, as I lay in bed trying to sleep, my worries about work were back. I decided right then that I would not be a grumpy husband and dad as our family grew. I knew I had to make a change, and I prayed that something would happen to make that possible. And, within a few months, those prayers were answered.

HEADHUNTER

I got a call one afternoon after my third frustrating meeting of the day. It was a guy from a staffing agency downtown.

"We've been following you for a while, Bull," the guy said.

I felt like a spy.

"One of the top agencies in the city would like to talk to you about a job. Would you be open to that?"

How could I not be? I mean, someone was following me, after all.

Two days later, I had lunch with a guy and a gal in a nice restaurant near the marina and learned that I could make almost 20 percent more money doing the same kind of work that I had been doing for years, and with more interesting clients.

So, I jumped. And landed well.

After four days of adjustment—yes, just four days—I was as happy as I had ever been in a job. New clients, new industries, new colleagues, and new ideas. And I still couldn't believe that changing jobs would lead to such a bump in my salary.

But compensation had little, if anything, to do with my sense of relief. I mean, I wasn't going to turn money down, but there was something else going on, something related to the job itself. I couldn't put my finger on it, so I just told myself and anyone who asked that I must really like advertising.

MONTAGE PART TWO

Fast-forward another seven years.

Anna had just given birth to our fourth child. By the way, none of them had names that sounded even remotely like a cow, or an animal of any kind. We had moved to a nice community called Pleasant Hill. And though life was moving faster than I would have liked, work was generally a source of joy.

Which reminds me, from time to time, I thought about Joy and the other tellers in the bank back home. Years earlier, during a trip to see my parents, I went through the drive-thru window to cash a check (people still did that then). I peeked inside and, to my dismay, saw Joy at her teller window, chatting away with a customer. Thankfully, she didn't see me because I didn't want to go inside and tell her how much happier I was now, devising advertising strategies instead of issuing cashier's checks. It would have been too sad for me. Or for her. I'm not sure.

So there I was, in the latter half of my thirties, doing my best to be a good husband and dad, enjoying my work more than I could have expected a decade earlier. To be fair, I had come to take my job satisfaction for granted. I had become a VP of something or other at the agency, and everything seemed to be going smoothly. Until the day of the announcement.

ACQUISITION

Mergers and buyouts within the world of advertising weren't all that rare back in the day, whatever that means. Bigger firms were buying smaller firms, and smaller firms were spinning off from bigger firms fairly regularly. So I wasn't particularly dismayed when we were purchased by one of the five largest agencies in the world.

We would keep most of our clients, and that was what seemed to matter most. But I didn't understand the impact of the larger company's operational model, and what it would mean for me personally.

I don't want to bore you with the details, but the new firm had a functional approach to client management rather than a geographical one. Essentially, that means that I had to collaborate with colleagues in New York and London who worked with clients in the same industry as mine. There was a hotel division. A consumer packaged goods division. A sports division. A sweet-and-spicy barbecue sauce division. Not really, but it sure seemed that way.

There were vice presidents all over the place, and I was one of them. And I have to say that, for the most part, they were generally well-intentioned people. The problem was that I had to meet with them constantly and use terms like *dotted lines* and *synergy* and *cross-functional buy-in* and *approval matrix*. It was mind-numbing. And deflating.

We wasted more time and seemed to get less accomplished during that time than at any point in my career. I had to play politics and get approvals at every step of the client process. And I couldn't protect my people from all of this. Based on their job descriptions, they had their own dotted lines to worry about, trying to survive the misery of matrix management. People couldn't step out of their lanes and had to figure out whether to please their boss, their functional teams around the world, or their clients. It was a mess.

And the worst part of all was that the firm's model seemed to work, at least from a financial standpoint. The mega-agency was making more money and drawing more new clients than any of their competitors. Who was I to argue with their approach? Besides, they were paying me, and my people, more than we ever expected or felt we deserved.

But for me, it wasn't enough. Because the Sunday Blues were back, and I decided that there wasn't enough money in the world to make me face those again.

CONFESSION

I knew I had to talk to Anna, and I wasn't looking forward to what she'd have to say. So I took her to our favorite little Italian restaurant, owned by a husband and wife from the same little town that her family came from in Tuscany. As much as I liked the food, I wanted her to be in a good mood when I broke the news.

I planned to wait until dessert.

"The Sunday Blues are back," I blurted out over burrata. I have so little self-control.

It took her a moment to digest what I was saying.

"Excuse me?" She was clearly unhappy.

"Yeah, I'm starting to dread going to work again."

Anna put down her fork and took a breath. "But you like Joe and Janet and the other guy with the J name." It seemed like an accusation more than a question or a statement of fact.

"Javier."

"Right," she said dispassionately. "I always forget him."

"Probably because his name seems like an H." I was trying to make a joke.

She didn't laugh, or even smile. "I guess so. Anyway, you said you like these people."

I nodded. "I do."

"Is it the woman from HR?"

"No." I laughed nervously. "Holly's a huge pain, but she's not enough to give me the Sunday Blues."

"Then what is it?" she asked, with a steely expression that I had only seen twice before, in situations that I'd prefer to forget.

"I don't know," I said, trying not to show fear. "I'm guessing it has something to do with the bureaucracy. The approvals. The reports. The virtual lack of anything creative."

Anna just sat there staring at her food for the longest fifteen seconds of my life.

Finally, taking a deep breath, she frowned and nodded her head just slightly but said nothing.

"What?" I asked.

"What what?" she countered coldly.

"Something's wrong," I declared. "I can tell something's wrong."

She took another deep breath and looked up and directly into my eyes. Something had changed. There was a subtle indication of empathy.

Finally, she spoke. "I think I know what you're thinking." She paused. "Even if you don't know that you're thinking it yet."

I had no idea what she meant, but I had grown accustomed to the accuracy of her spousal telepathy.

Still scared, I responded, "What am I thinking?"

"I'll let you figure it out," she declared before taking a bite of burrata.

"That's not fair," I pleaded unsuccessfully, trying pathetically to lighten the mood. "You know me better than I do."

Our food arrived, which provided a few minutes of distraction so that I could catch up with my wife's brain and gather my courage.

After an avalanche of parmesan cheese had fallen onto my pasta and the man with the grater left the table, I continued. "So, you're saying I'm thinking something, and you don't like it?"

"Partially correct," she announced flatly as she carefully took a bite of hot gnocchi.

"So, you *do* like what I'm thinking, which I don't even know I'm thinking?"

I think she almost smiled, but I couldn't be sure. "I don't dislike it. It's just not easy for me."

"So it's a big change."

She looked up at me and nodded just slightly. Now there was the faintest hint of a tear in her eyes.

And that's when it dawned on me.

Lowering my voice, not because anyone would hear me but because I was almost afraid to say the words out loud, I spoke. "I should start my own firm."

Anna closed her eyes, and slowly nodded.

After another ten seconds of silence, I asked, "And you'd be okay with that?"

"No," she said matter-of-factly.

I was confused.

"But I'm convinced it's the only way that you're going to be happy at work." She paused yet again, took a bite of her food, swallowed, and continued. "And I think it's time we relocated. This is the right time for all of this, for you, for me, for the kids."

I took a breath and was about to speak, but she answered my question before I could.

"Yes, I'm sure."

BAND-AID

Several months later, we were living on the Nevada side of Lake Tahoe, just a dozen miles away from the chaos of a state where we had lived all our lives. I found a rustic office with a view of Mt. Rose, and had no problem recruiting a few staff members, friends, and former colleagues who were more eager to escape than I had realized.

Being out of a major metropolitan area—no offense, Reno—wasn't a problem given that most of what we did was digital. We had also become early adopters of video technology for meetings and collaboration with clients.

We called the firm Jeremiah Marketing—the group insisted that we find a way to use my name, which had been hidden from the world for the past forty-two years. Thirty minutes from the lake, the ski slopes, and an international airport gave us just the right feel. Everything felt lighter, and it wasn't just the altitude.

The office consisted of twelve people. I was CEO, whatever that meant. I should probably give you a rundown of my executive team, because most of what happens next involves them.

Amy Sample was the VP of sales and client relations. I had met her years earlier in the first ad firm where I worked. She didn't work on the Llama Project with Jasper and me, but she started on one of the lower rungs of the ladder like us, and she was a gem.

Chris Herrera, a friend of mine from college who studied economics and actually remembered some of it, ran finance, operations, and all things administrative. We called him the CFO. I trusted him with my life and knew that I would never have to lose sleep over payroll, AR, or financial solvency. I hugged him regularly.

Quinn Ryder was a butt-kicking young woman recommended by Amy, and she did a little bit of everything. I knew she'd be the utility infielder, if you're a baseball fan, or perhaps the glue that held everything together when the proverbial shit hit the fan. How's that for mixing metaphors? Anyway, Quinn handled advertising purchases and operational services for clients, and anything else that others needed.

And then there was Jasper Jones, my partner at the petting zoo. Like most guys, we did a poor job of staying in touch after parting ways years earlier but picked up like no time had gone by when I approached him about joining the firm. He had grown one of those longish beards since I had last seen him, which seemed to fit in nicely with our new gig in the mountains. Jasper was VP of Services. He helped me with client solutions but had developed something of a specialty in digital advertising and social media.

Oh, and I almost forgot to mention Lynne Lynn. That's her name. I kid you not. She was originally Lynne Gregory but fell in love and married a great guy with an unfortunate last name, causing her to spend the last fifteen years convincing people not to call her LynneLynn. We call her that anyway. Lynne is our creative director, focusing on artistic design, layout, and production.

We had a half dozen others in the office who did a variety of important things at a slightly lower level. To be fair, we all did our share of grunt work, which is how it works in a small firm. I like it that way.

Anyway, our office was nice, with lots of light and windows. But it was not pretentious like so many ad agencies we had worked with. There were no ladders or beanbag chairs or tables for foosball, Ping-Pong, or massages, though we always had beer and Dr Pepper in the fridge.

Everything at JM, as we called it, was wonderful for the first two years. At home, too, thank God. But that's a different (and more important) story.

Our slightly remote location wasn't a barrier for us getting great clients from all over the country, and we were making a bit more money than we had expected, which went a lot further with lower taxes and a sane cost of living. We continued to attract good people as we grew, finding more solid talent in the local area than we had expected. Most important of all, everyone was having a heck of a lot of fun.

Unfortunately, as we began the third year in our start-up venture, something changed. I caught a case of, as I would later call it, "the crankies."

THE CRANKIES

They were nothing like the Sunday Blues, because I never dreaded work during the weekends, and I was happy to go to the office on Mondays and every other morning. After all, I was working with people who had been, or who had become, close friends. We did interesting work, did it well, and were recognized for making a difference for our clients.

But somehow, with increasing frequency, I found myself more stressed and—what's the right word?—more irritable than I should have been. I'd get short with people once a week or so, wearing that look on my face that made them think I was slightly disgusted with them. And then it started happening more often.

At first, people teased me about it. Jasper started referring to the way I looked when I got frustrated as "the face." He even did a hilarious impression of me, which hurt a little more than I let on. One day at home, Anna inadvertently came up with a rapper name for me when she said, "You're a little harsh, aren't you? We should call you Lil' Harsh." I shouldn't have told the youngsters at work, because from that moment on, they adopted the label.

As funny as that was, the reality of my irritability was a problem I didn't understand. How could a guy who ran his own firm, surrounded by wonderful people, be so temperamental?

As desperate as I was to solve my dilemma, Anna was even more determined. "You better figure this out, Bull. We're not moving again, and you're never going to find a better group to work with if you piss them off." She probably used kinder words than that, but it's how I like to remember it.

Thank God for Amy, who unknowingly provoked a discovery that would change my career, our team, and my life.

THE QUESTION

We were doing a sales pitch to a local company called Reno-Corp that owned a minor league baseball team, a hockey team, and an events center in the area. A really cool organization.

Though there were a few typos and glitches in our presentation, Amy and I pulled it off, and it looked like we would have a new client. But on the way back to the office, I vented about the mistakes that Makena and Shane, two of our younger employees, had made in preparing our pitch. I guess I was pretty angry, even using a few choice words, which Anna accused me of doing more and more recently.

When we got back to the office, I called Shane and Makena in for a debrief with Amy and me, and I scolded them for the errors in their work. I wasn't too harsh, Amy later assured me. "Not even lil' harsh," she joked. But I was clearly annoyed that I had to tell these guys that their oversights could have jeopardized our pitch.

As soon as the admonished youngsters slunk out of the room, I turned to Amy.

"Hey, I've got an idea for the new resort we're pitching up in Graeagle. It's a family-oriented place, and we should do something that contrasts with the Las Vegas thing. *What happens at Graeagle shouldn't stay at Graeagle. Take home a lifetime of memories.* Something like that."

Amy looked at me strangely.

"What?" I wanted to know.

"Why are you like this?" she asked rhetorically.

"What do you mean?"

"I don't know." She frowned, in a kind but curious way. "Thirty seconds ago, you were exasperated. Now you're lit up around a new idea."

I wasn't clear what she meant, so she went on. "You go from frustrated to inspired in seconds, and I'd like to know what causes that." She actually seemed to be waiting for a response this time.

"You're right," I admitted. "You're completely right. I wish I understood why."

After a pause, she started gathering her things to leave.

I stopped her. "No, I really wish I understood why. Half the time, I'm psyched about work. Half the time, I'm frustrated. And half the time, I'm confused by it all."

"You can't have three halves."

"What?"

She smiled. "You said 'half the time' three times."

I laughed. "Shut up. I feel a little crazy here. Throw me a bone."

Amy put her bag back down on the floor. "Okay, but first I have to tell you something that I've never said before."

My eyes went wide. "Okay."

She took a deep breath. "About six months ago, I got a call from that PR firm down in Reno. They wanted to hire me."

I wasn't flustered by her comment. "Why didn't you tell me? It's not that big of a deal unless—"

She interrupted me. "I actually interviewed there and thought about taking the job."

Now I was flustered. Or, perhaps, stunned.

Before I could ask why, Amy explained. "These ups and downs you go through can get pretty exhausting. I wondered if it might be more"—she paused, trying to think of the right word—"more steady and calm somewhere else."

Recovering from my surprise, I asked her, "So what happened?"

"After one interview, I realized that I wouldn't have as much fun there, and that I would miss you and the team way too much."

I gladly received her response but couldn't shake the idea that she had even entertained the thought of leaving.

"So . . ." I took a breath. "Figuring this out is a pretty big deal."

She smiled and nodded her head. "Yeah, I think so."

We sat there for a long ten seconds.

"Let's do this," Amy announced, and we dove in.

In spite of my surprise at what Amy had told me, I have to admit that the next three hours flew by in a blur. In fact, I feel like I blacked out at eleven and woke up at two because, to this day, I have a hard time remembering exactly what happened. Amy, as well as Jasper and Lynne, who eventually joined us, assure me that I was, indeed, involved.

BLUR

First, Amy and I talked for about a half hour. I explained to her that I would often come into work happy and excited about the day, and then something would happen that would send me off into exasperation.

"I know it's not the people that are the problem," I explained. "You guys are terrific. And I'm not in a generally bad mood in the morning. Anna will tell you that I leave for the office in a good place. But by noon, I'm complaining and feeling somehow suddenly exhausted."

Amy winced. "You're not just complaining." She paused. "You're kind of angry."

That hurt. But I couldn't argue.

At that moment, Jasper and Lynne came into the room. Before they could ask a question about the morning's client presentation, I was pressing them for information.

"Why do you think I've been getting grumpy so much lately?"

"Because you're an asshole," Jasper offered without hesitation.

As desperate as I was to figure this out, I couldn't help but laugh. Neither could Lynne and Amy. Jasper was funny.

"Other than that," I played along. "What is it that pushes me from joyful to agitated?"

Jasper sat down at the table, more serious now, and shrugged. "I don't know. You must have some idea."

Lynne joined in. "What do you say about it to Anna when you get home at night?"

"Great question," I responded and thought about it for a moment. "I tell her that I'm tired."

"Tired?" Lynne asked. "Or tired of something?"

She hit a nerve.

"Tired of something," I agreed and thought about it for a few more moments.

"Of what?" Lynne persisted.

Suddenly I felt excited. "I always tell her that I'm tired of having to constantly check on things and keep them moving forward, and feeling like if I don't, things will grind to a halt."

People's eyes widened, as though we might have discovered something helpful.

"But that's your job," Jasper said.

"Yeah, I know. But I really wish I didn't have to do it so much. I want to be the fun guy. I don't want to be the pusher."

"What do you mean by 'the fun guy'?" Jasper asked.

"You know. The guy who comes up with new ideas. Who evaluates different ideas and figures out the best ones."

"That's not the fun guy job," Jasper said. "That sounds miserable."

I was genuinely surprised. "What's more fun than that?"

Jasper thought about it. "When a client calls about something at the last minute and I get to be their hero, that's fun. And when they ask me for something impossible, and I come through for them so well that they call me the next day to say that I saved their butt."

I was shocked. "That's my nightmare! No wonder I love working with you. I never have to do that." Then something hit me. "Do you like to exhort people?"

Jasper seemed unclear about what I was asking.

I clarified. "To keep them moving forward, and make sure they're engaged and on track?" Before he could respond, I answered for him, somewhat accusingly. "You don't like that, do you?"

Jasper shook his head. "I wouldn't say I don't like it." Before I could object, he finished. "I'd say I hate it." He explained. "I'd rather just do the work myself."

Amy chimed in. "Me, too."

Lynne raised her hand in agreement.

"Shit," I said, using one of those "choice" words again. "I'm the only exhorter."

DRILLING

Explain more about that," Lynne requested.

I was getting excited. "No one else here likes to keep people from losing momentum. Exhort them to keep going."

"I think Chris does that sometimes," Amy countered.

I thought about it. "Yeah, but only around admin and financial stuff," I explained. "I think I'm the one who does it around just about everything else."

"But you're good at it," Lynne insisted. "We like when you exhort us, if that's what you call it."

"But I don't. It wipes me out. When I come to work, I'm thinking about some new project or problem we're going to solve that day, and then—"

Jasper interrupted. "And then I tell you we're starting to fall behind on online content."

"Right!" I cried out. "And I have to start asking questions and convincing people to get excited again. I feel like I might be frustrating everyone. And I know I'm frustrated myself."

"But we almost always end up doing it better," Jasper defended, "and we always hit our targets."

"But why don't *you* exhort them?" I asked Jasper, in a slightly agitated way.

"You've got that angry face again," he informed me.

"I'm sorry. And thank you for telling me." I took a breath and chose my words carefully. "I don't mean this as a criticism. I'm just curious as to why you let me do it."

Jasper frowned. "I guess I know that you're better at it than me. And, to be honest, I thought you liked it. It seems easy for you."

Amy looked at me and winced. "Me, too."

Jasper went on. "I guess we've just always seen you as being the Chief Exhorting Officer."

We laughed.

"Well, I'm becoming the Chief Pissed-Off Officer, and that's not good for me or anyone else."

"So, what do we do?" he asked.

And, according to everyone in the room, that was the moment I went to the whiteboard, and the circles began to emerge.

INCREMENTALISM

Time flies when I have a marker in my hand.

From what everyone tells me, we spent less than five minutes discussing my mood swings and shifted to the process of work. We analyzed the difference between what happens at the beginning of a project and at the end, and how we were drawn to work at different stages. And I am being completely serious when I say that, for some reason, I can't recall all the details about that conversation, but I do know that it was intensely fun.

Within ninety minutes, the whiteboard in our conference room was covered with words and shapes and arrows. In the center of it all were three circles arranged horizontally.

Above the first circle, I had written the word *ideation*, and above the third was *implementation*. The middle circle is what we found most fascinating, or perhaps novel, and above it was the word *activation*. We labeled this the "Three Stages of Work."

THREE STAGES OF WORK

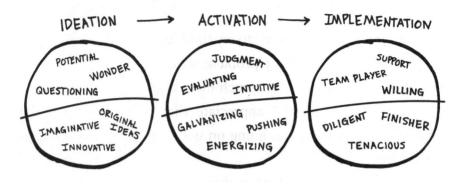

Each circle was filled with half a dozen other words to describe what it meant. We added and subtracted words every time we checked our thesauruses and found something better. We divided the circles into halves and shoved some words into one half versus the other. It was a mess, and we needed to step back from it all in order to go any further. We were kind of stuck.

So, we did what we always did in these situations: We brought new people into the room. In this case, Chris, our CFO, and Quinn, the utility player. We call these progressive meetings, which involves having to stop and explain a new idea to new people from scratch. There are two benefits.

First, having to re-explain the idea allows the original team to get clear with one another about what they decided, even allowing them to iterate while they present to new people. Second, and more obvious, it provides a source of fresh, new input.

As soon as Chris and Quinn arrived, I dove in. I remember this part vividly.

"Okay, I was venting again to Amy about why I'm tired and grumpy and all that stuff."

They nodded, accustomed to my thinking out loud with people.

"She asked me what my problem was, and—"

Amy interrupted. "I was much nicer than that."

I agreed. "Yes, and I appreciate that. But essentially, she wanted to know what was going on with me. I was kind of hoping she knew."

I went to the whiteboard at that moment and pointed to the lower half of the middle circle, where the words *pushing* and *energizing* and *galvanizing* were written.

"She didn't have an answer, but in the course of our conversation, this is what we came up with."

Amy corrected me kindly. "What *you* came up with."

"Well, we were both involved in the conversation."

Before Amy could argue that point, Quinn spoke up. "What exactly does *galvanizing* mean?"

"Great question," I said. "It's about getting people moving. Keeping them moving. Rallying people and getting them to commit and recommit and commit again."

Chris jumped in. "I'm confused. What do the circles represent? I need some context here."

He was right, which was probably why I said, "You're right." I'm smart that way.

So I grabbed the eraser, but before I could remove the writing from the whiteboard, Lynne was snapping pictures with her phone so we wouldn't lose what we'd done.

I decided to start from the beginning.

THE WHOLE ENCHILADA

By now, it was almost one o'clock and we hadn't eaten lunch. And because I wanted to get Chris's and Quinn's full attention, I suggested we bring in food and clear out the rest of the afternoon. After everyone had made a few calls and confirmed that they were available—I have to admit that I begged them—we dug in.

"So, my frustration is not with the company, or with you guys, or with clients," I explained. "It's something much more fundamental."

I paused, not for effect but because I wanted to use the right words. "It has to do with doing work that drains me of my energy, and which, in turn, prevents me from doing the work that gives me energy."

Quinn's eyes went wide, and I could tell she was hooked. Chris frowned, not there yet.

I began. "There are three stages of work, I think."

"Wait," Chris interrupted. "What kind of work are we talking about here?"

Amy jumped in before I could. "Anything from starting a company, or running a project, or"—she thought about it—"planning your family's vacation."

I hadn't thought about the vacation thing, but it made sense. I explained. "It's about getting things done. Anything."

Chris nodded, not so much to say he understood it all, but to give us permission to go on.

"The first stage we call ideation." I drew the first circle.

Now Quinn spoke. "Is that innovation?"

"Sure," I allowed. "We like ideation because I think all of our work involves innovation. But the initial idea has to start somewhere." I was determined to lay out the model. "We'll come back to that in a second. Let me get through the three circles."

"Oh, I'm sorry," Quinn apologized.

"No," I reassured her. "I love your curiosity. I just want to unveil the whole thing so you can go to town on it in a few minutes."

She seemed relieved, and I continued.

"The third circle"—I drew it over to the right—"is implementation. This is where we get things done. That's pretty clear, right?"

Everyone nodded, including the folks who had been involved in the original conversation, which told me they were kind of recommitting to the model.

"Where's the second circle?" Chris asked.

"Hold your horses, Herrera," Jasper teased. "He's getting to that right now."

Everything sounds funnier when Jasper says it, so we cracked up.

"The second circle is the one that we don't think about much, and that's one of the things that's so exciting here." I drew the second circle, between the other two. "We're calling it activation."

Both Quinn and Chris frowned a little, displaying curiosity, not disagreement.

Lynne finally jumped in. "You can't just come up with new ideas and then start implementing them."

"Why not?" Quinn wanted to know.

"Well," Lynne allowed, "I guess you can, but it doesn't work very well. What if your ideas are terrible or not complete?"

"Isn't that the implementers' job to fix?" she asked.

Lynne shook her head. "No. The implementers are cranking. They need to know that what they're doing has already been vetted."

Quinn pushed a little more. "Then why don't the ideators do that?"

I jumped in. "They're not necessarily good at that. And I'm pretty sure they're focused on coming up with new ideas, not evaluating whether those ideas would work."

"And that's what the middle circle is?" Chris asked. "They figure out if a new idea is good?"

I hesitated. "Yeah, but it's more than that. Let me explain what happens within each of these three stages."

Quinn winced. "I'm sorry, guys, but I'm not seeing how this explains why Bull is pissed off so much."

I was glad that it was Jasper who answered her. He was uncharacteristically serious. "You will. It's going to explain a lot."

Quinn's demeanor changed immediately. "Okay. You've got my attention."

This prompted Chris to say something that no one expected. "I love this shit."

Everyone, including me, was surprised.

Chris explained. "I could talk about this stuff all day."

To my delight, the energy in the room surged as a result of the unexpected comment.

And then something occurred to Jasper. "Hey, this is Bullshit." People were confused. He pointed at me. "Bull." Then he pointed at the board. "Shit. Bull shit."

If anyone else had said it, we would have groaned. But there was something about Jasper, and we were laughing again.

I was just psyched that people were interested.

REFINEMENT

I kept the conversation moving. "So, here at work, we have to ideate, activate, and implement. They're all equally important, but it starts with ideation, which is my favorite part."

Suddenly, Amy was confused.

"Wait a second, Bull. I think I'm good at ideation, but I don't come up with new ideas like you do."

I stared at the circles for a few long seconds. I was puzzled. "It seems like you're almost always part of the ideation process. I mean, you're the person I brainstorm with the most. Maybe you're more inventive and creative than you think."

She frowned. "No, I'm definitely not creative. I've never been." She thought about it some more. "I just like having my. head up there in the clouds with you."

I was starting to worry that our little model was unraveling when Lynne spoke up. "Maybe coming up with a new idea is not the first step in ideation."

She had our attention and didn't need to wait until we asked why.

"Someone has to identify the problem"—she paused—"or the opportunity, first."

I think if it weren't for Amy's dilemma, I would have disagreed. But after considering it for a few seconds, I realized she was right. "The first part of ideation is about asking and pondering and wondering and posing the questions."

"What questions?" Jasper wanted to know.

"The big questions, the ones Amy is always asking. 'Why is it this way?' 'Is there a better way?' 'Is there more potential here?' Those are the questions that come before anyone can start inventing."

To my surprise, and everyone else's, Chris went to the board, erased the first circle, and wrote two of them in its place. "Doesn't this make more sense? There are two different activities and skills involved here."

"But they're both part of ideation," Lynne said.

"I'm just saying," Chris explained in his rational and compelling way, "that you might as well separate the two halves because they're not the same thing. It's confusing."

I took the eraser from Chris—who seemed just a little concerned—and removed the other two circles and replaced them with four. We had six now: two each in ideation, activation, and implementation.

"So, you're just assuming that there are two in each category?" Jasper asked. "Maybe we shouldn't jump to conclusions."

I smiled. "We can always erase, my friend."

And then everything came to a crashing halt when Bella, our office manager, came in to take our food orders.

MESSY BREAKTHROUGH

When we had all finished debating the difference between carne asada and barbacoa, we turned back to the whiteboard. The six circles stared at us.

"I still don't know why, or if, there are six," Jasper began. "Let's forget about the shapes and arrows and just figure out how work gets done."

I liked his suggestion, and so did everyone else. So Jasper took over.

"Let's think about a client project. What was the company you guys pitched today?"

"RenoCorp," Amy responded.

"Are they the company that runs the sports teams and the big arena west of the airport?" Chris asked.

Jasper nodded and pushed on. "Okay, how did this project get started?"

I looked at Amy. "It was your idea, right?"

"I think so. I was just wondering why so many of our clients are on the other side of the mountains, or the other side of the country. And I was watching a Jokers hockey game the other night with Dan, and the next day I asked Bull why we shouldn't try to make them a client."

No one said anything, so she kept going.

"The next thing I know, Bull has a mock-up of ads that they could run in Tahoe and in the airport, and an idea about sponsoring schools in the area. And he starts thinking about partnerships with St. Luke's Hospital, especially the orthopedic unit that deals with injuries and rehab."

I jumped in. "To be fair, Lynne helped me with the ads."

"Yeah," she acknowledged, "but you had three drawings and a handful of slogans before I knew what was going on. I just told you which ones were good, which were dogs, and made you tweak some of what you brought me. I don't know what that is, but it comes after the ideation."

"It's called good taste," Chris declared.

"Or intuition," I added, pointing to the board. "Judgment and instinct and discernment. And it provides feedback to the person who does the creative invention. You helped me, like you always do, avoid going too far with a bad idea—or one that's not quite ready."

Lynne seemed flattered by my comment, though that wasn't my intention. It was just true.

I went to the whiteboard, completed those first two circles, and wrote those words in the third circle.

Lynne summarized. "So the first thing is to question or ponder or wonder about something. The second is to create or invent a solution or a new idea. The third is to"—she paused, trying to

THREE STAGES OF WORK

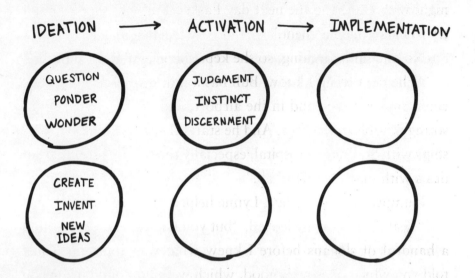

IDEATION ⟶ ACTIVATION ⟶ IMPLEMENTATION

QUESTION
PONDER
WONDER

JUDGMENT
INSTINCT
DISCERNMENT

CREATE
INVENT
NEW
IDEAS

summarize the discussion we had just had—"evaluate and assess whether it's a good idea."

"I like the word *discernment*," Amy offered. "It's more about having good judgment and gut feel than being smart."

"Are you saying I'm not smart?" teased Lynne.

"That's the way I heard it," Jasper joked, deadpan as always.

Quinn was staring at the board and didn't seem to hear the joke. "I have to tell you guys something." She paused and let the laughter fade out. "This makes sense to me. And it explains a lot."

"Tell me again how it explains why Bull is always pissed off," Lynne requested.

"Hey," I protested. "I'm not pissed off *all* the time."

"That's not what I meant. I should have said—"

I interrupted her. "I know. I'm just kidding."

Quinn continued. "So, is this where the galvanizing thing comes into play?"

Amy answered. "I think so. Once we feel that an idea or a proposal or a plan is good, we need to get people fired up about it."

And that's when a light bulb went on in my head.

CRANKY TRIGGER

I just realized something. Just because you're good at a task or an activity doesn't mean you like doing it all the time. I can galvanize and push people pretty well, but I don't enjoy it. After a while, if I have to do it too much, it drains me, and I get discouraged."

"But what if you're the best we have at doing it?" asked Jasper. "And besides, who gets to spend all their time doing things they like?"

"Well . . ." I thought about it. "Don't get me wrong. Everyone has parts of their job that we don't like. We all have to suck it up sometimes."

People seemed to be relieved that I wasn't arguing for some sort of utopian idealism. "But, if my experience is any indication, if you have to do those things too often, you're probably going to be pretty unpleasant. Or a little harsh."

"So, I guess we're screwed," declared Jasper dryly.

"Pretty much," I teased back.

Quinn was frowning now. "Maybe we don't need a galvanizer."

Amy frowned, thinking, and finally shook her head. "No. If Bull doesn't galvanize us, we won't get half as much done. We need pushing."

"See? Screwed," repeated Jasper.

"Maybe we just have to get used to Bull being grumpy," Quinn offered unenthusiastically.

Amy shook her head. "No, that doesn't work. Aside from it being unfair to him and unpleasant for the rest of us, we'll end up losing the things we really need him to do, and the stuff that makes him happy."

"Explain what you like again," Jasper asked me in another rare moment of seriousness.

I walked over to the whiteboard. "I like inventing things, and evaluating things." I pointed at the second and third circles.

Jasper stared at the board. "Invention makes sense. I like that word. But I think Amy's right. We should call the other one *discernment*. Those are your geniuses."

"Geniuses?" Lynne asked. "What do you mean?"

"You know." Jasper seemed surprised by the question. "Your genius. Your talent. The things you're world-class in. Bull is a genius inventor and discerner."

Chris and Quinn were nodding their heads.

Jasper went on. "But he's not a genius at pushing, which is why we're screwed."

"Don't give up yet," Amy chided him playfully. "We can figure something out."

PUSHING

I wanted to make the situation seem a little more hopeful. "So, I get grumpy when I have to get people refocused all the time. That's not an insurmountable problem."

"But isn't that your job as CEO?" Quinn pushed.

"Hey, that's what *I* said," Jasper bragged.

Lynne clarified. "Well, it's Bull's job to make sure our goals are clear and that we're motivated to get them done. But the fact is, the rest of us don't like to exhort, so we just let him do all of it."

Chris suddenly seemed surprised. He turned to me and asked, "And it really bothers you to have to do that, Bull?"

I nodded slowly and earnestly. "Oh yeah. It wipes me out."

People were taking it all in, so I continued. "Like I was telling Amy, I leave for work excited to come up with creative ideas, and I like using my judgment to evaluate other people's ideas. And then I walk in the door, and I feel like I've got to push the proverbial ball uphill to keep people focused. I didn't realize it until a few hours ago, but it's been destroying my passion for work. And not just now. That's how it's been for years. Now I understand why I got the Sunday Blues so many times earlier in my career."

At that point, I had to explain to Lynne what the Sunday Blues were.

And that's when Chris just started laughing. We turned to him, more than a little curious.

With a mixture of passion and just a bit of frustration, he declared, "Well, hell, I *like* doing that!" He paused, looking at the whiteboard again. "It's my favorite part of work, and I wish you'd let me do more of it."

Everyone was silent, but in an anticipatory kind of way.

"Tell me more about that," I asked him.

"Well, I'm always feeling like I have to stay in my swim lane and keep my focus on administrative and financial stuff. I don't want to step on anyone's toes around client work and schedules, and so I bite my lip."

"Really?" Lynne replied.

"Really what?" Chris countered. "Do I like exhorting people, or do I feel like I'm not supposed to step outside my area?"

Lynne smiled, a little unsure of how to answer. "You feel like we don't want you in our part of the business?"

Chris hesitated for a moment, then nodded. "Yeah."

She continued. "And you'd like to be more involved?"

Chris nodded his head. "Oh yeah."

"Well, hallelujah!" I exclaimed. "I've got myself a Chief Exhorting Officer."

SPECIFICS

Chris couldn't stop smiling but seemed a little hesitant all of a sudden. "Whoa, hold on a minute. What have I got myself into here?"

I announced, "Everything!"

Even Jasper laughed.

I continued. "You're going to be involved in virtually every single thing we do, but mostly in terms of rallying the troops and making sure that we're not losing steam."

"How much time is that going to require?" he wanted to know.

"As much as it takes," I assured him. "But not as much as you think. And here's the thing." I paused for effect. "It's going to be so much fun that you won't even worry about that."

Now Amy was confused. "I'm not clear what that means."

"Neither am I," I responded joyfully. "But that's okay. Chris is just going to have permission . . ." I hesitated. "No, he's going to have *responsibility* for checking in with us and keeping us on track."

Amy frowned and directed her next question at me. "And you're not going to do that at all?"

"I'll have to do *some* of it. I mean, I have to be Chris's Chief Exhorting Officer. And if he's not seeing enough energy or movement, I have to be willing to step in and help him. But remember, he *likes* exhorting, galvanizing, keeping things moving, and now he gets to do it a hell of a lot more."

Something clicked, and Chris was suddenly smiling. "When can I start?"

There was a palpable sense of relief in the room.

Jasper stood up and put his hands in the air. "We're not completely screwed!"

Everyone laughed yet again.

"Right now," I said, looking at Chris. "I declare you the new Chief Exhorting Officer."

"Could I be the Chief Galvanizing Officer instead? Otherwise, I sound like I'm the CEO."

"Galvanizing is better anyway," Lynne confirmed.

"Galvanizing it is," I agreed, and we decided to take a break.

ORDER

By the time we returned, Chris was standing at the whiteboard. He had erased everything and redrawn the circles more neatly.

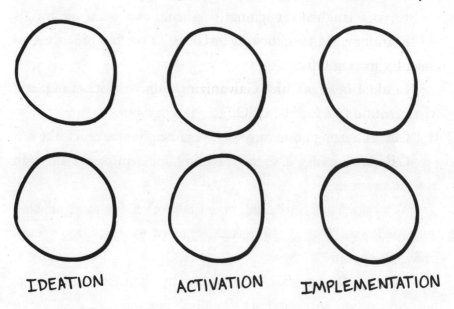

IDEATION   ACTIVATION   IMPLEMENTATION

"Now that's what I'm talking about," I declared when I saw the board. "I love that you're grabbing the pen and taking charge."

"Well," Chris replied. "If I don't get you guys moving, we'll be here through dinner."

And at that moment, Jasper came into the room with two bags filled with Mexican food.

Chris winced. "Oh boy. There goes our productivity."

I disagreed. "No. I'll get everyone's food. You keep us moving."

Two minutes later, everyone was sitting at the table, and Chris was facilitating. I was making sense of the food for them.

"So, how many of these different skills does a person have?" Amy asked, looking at me as I unwrapped burritos and tortillas.

I shrugged. "Well, we're still figuring out what all this is about, so it's hard to say." I was staring at the board, trying to come up with an idea.

Quinn jumped in. "If it's about the things you love doing, and that give you energy, I can't imagine having more than a couple. If it's about getting good at something, even if you don't like doing it, I'd have to say it varies. Some people can power through almost anything."

"Why don't we finish the model before we try to figure that out," protested Jasper. "Because, according to this, I don't think I have any geniuses."

I agreed. "Remember, we're flying by the seat of our pants here, folks, and without a net. We don't even—"

Jasper interrupted. "What kind of analogy is that? What the heck does a net have to do with flying?"

I threw a rolled-up ball of foil at him. "You know what I mean."

Chris took over. "So, Amy's good at wondering."

She jumped in. "That's not my only skill."

"Right," Chris allowed. "But that's at least one of yours. And Bull is good at invention and discernment."

"Discernment is one of my geniuses, too," Lynne declared. "My husband says I have great instincts and gut feel."

We acknowledged her husband's assessment with immediate nods and comments.

Chris wrote people's names next to the circles on the board and announced, "And apparently, I'm the only one who likes to galvanize and push people."

"What's next?" asked Amy.

"Why do there have to be any others?" Quinn asked.

"Because work doesn't stop with galvanizing," I explained. "And poor Jasper doesn't have any geniuses yet."

"So, what happens after someone galvanizes?" Amy posed the question.

After a brief pause, Lynne responded. "That's implementation. Someone has to respond to whatever the galvanizer is galvanizing them around."

"Like volunteer?" I asked.

Quinn winced. "That sounds so"—she searched for a word—"weak. I mean, volunteering isn't a genius, is it?"

Now Chris spoke. "I think it is. I mean, it's not really volunteering as much as it is being the first person to stop what they're doing and get something new off the ground. Some of the best employees I've ever managed were so good at coming to the rescue when an emergency happened. Or even without an emergency, when anyone needed help with an important project or program, those same people would always step up and make the work possible."

"I'm one of those," Jasper announced flatly. "That's me."

Almost at once, Quinn and Lynne and Amy said "absolutely" or "completely" or "that's Jasper in a nutshell."

I chimed in. "As much of a pain in the ass as you are, Jasper, you are always ready to help and to do what is needed without a bunch of fanfare."

"I'm low maintenance," he announced proudly.

And once again, a chorus of "absolutely" and "no doubt" and other phrases were spoken.

People were pointing at Quinn. "You're one of those, too," someone said.

We all agreed, and Quinn seemed both embarrassed and proud at once.

"But what do we call this one?" asked Amy. "The genius of volunteering? Or support?"

"That makes me sound like my mother," Quinn complained. "Not that I don't love my mother. But being a good helper or supporter doesn't sound very important or special."

Chris became almost defensive. "I disagree completely."

Everyone was suddenly silent, and Chris was the center of attention.

The CFO and newly minted CGO explained. "I hate to admit this, but I am absolutely terrible at this one. If I didn't have people in my life, at work and at home, who were helpers or supporters, I wouldn't be able to get anything done. These people are lifesavers."

"Maybe we should call me a lifesaver," Jasper offered, sarcastically. "I like that."

I jumped in again. "I think Jasper and Quinn and people like them are the ones who enable others to be successful. *That* is their genius." I turned to Amy. "Remember Rhonda at the Broadmoor Agency?"

Amy nodded enthusiastically. "Everyone wanted Rhonda on their team because she made sure they succeeded."

"And it was never about her," I added. "She enabled everyone and everything around her to work."

"Was she an administrative assistant?" Jasper asked.

"No, she was an account manager just like Amy and me. And though she wasn't the best at coming up with new strategies or ideas, I would have paid her more than anyone because she was the secret weapon on our teams."

Quinn protested again. "But that word, *enablement*, sounds like a bad thing you do for an alcoholic or a drug addict."

A few people agreed.

"But who cares?" Chris announced confidently. "Outside of that, it's really what this is about. It's not support or help or being nice. It's about enabling things to get off the ground. I wish I were an enabler."

"Really?" Quinn asked.

"Yes," he insisted passionately. "And so does my wife." He hadn't intended it as a joke, but we cracked up.

He went on. "I just don't find it easy to give people what they need on their terms. It's a huge struggle when it comes to getting involved at church or at my kids' schools. I'm a terrible enabler, which makes me feel like an absolute jerk!"

Suddenly, Quinn smiled. "Oh my gosh. I'm a total enabler. I'm the best volunteer, committee member—"

I interrupted. "And team player."

"Ladies and gentlemen, we have a winner." Chris turned to the board and wrote down Quinn's name and Jasper's name next to a circle labeled with the word *enablement*.

"And Jasper finally has a genius!" Lynne announced.

"I'm not a loser after all!" he celebrated.

"Does this bring us to the end of our little model?" asked Chris.

Everyone paused, looking at the whiteboard, and at one another.

After a long seven seconds, something clicked for me. "I think I have it."

"Let's hear it," someone said. I think it was Lynne.

"Enablers aren't finishers," I declared, somewhat controversially.

"What do you mean?" Jasper wanted to know. He seemed just slightly annoyed. Or maybe offended.

"Just because you're an enabler," I explained carefully, "doesn't mean you like to complete things, to get them across the finish line."

"That sounds like galvanizing," Quinn said.

I clarified. "No. Galvanizing is inspiring and motivating others—the organization, peers—to rally around something and keep moving. This is different." I hesitated as I searched for the right way to explain what I was thinking. "Some people don't like to push people, but they live for finishing projects and seeing them completed. They actually lose their energy if they're not allowed to see things through, even in the face of obstacles. They're geniuses at finishing things and maintaining high standards."

Jasper sat up in his chair. "I think you're wrong. I love to finish things." Again, there was a subtle but unmistakable sense of defensiveness in his tone.

The room was suddenly silent. Until Quinn spoke.

"I hate finishing things." If the room hadn't been so quiet, we might not have heard it. But given the awkwardness of the moment, she might as well have screamed it.

"What do you mean?" asked Jasper, almost annoyed.

"I love helping people, enabling them to succeed. That's definitely my genius." She paused. "But I lose my energy when it comes to the last ten percent of a project. As long as people are not in distress, I'll move on to something else. Heck, I don't even know half the time if what I was working on ever landed."

Jasper looked at her seriously. "You, my dear, are a freak."

It was clearly one of Jasper's dry attempts at humor, and as usual, it worked. We howled.

Jasper kept going. "But don't you want to see it through to the end?"

She smiled sheepishly, and slowly shook her head. "I know

I'm an enabler, and though I didn't say it earlier, I think I'm a discerner, too. I just keep my opinions to myself. But I'm not at all tenacious about wrestling things to the ground."

Jasper just shook his head in mock disgust at Quinn, who threw a tortilla chip at him.

Chris addressed his next pronouncement at Jasper. "So you have the genius of enablement and finishing." He wrote Jasper's name next to the circle.

"It's more than finishing," Lynne said. "Like Quinn said, it's about wrestling things to the ground when they are unruly. It's pushing—the work, not the people—until the goal is met. There has to be a better word."

"It's tenacity," Quinn declared. "Jasper is tenacious. So is Chris."

Chris nodded his head. "I didn't want to say anything, but I think that's one of my geniuses, too. My old boss used to say I was tenacious. My wife says it, too, though she's not always praising me for it."

"Yeah, you're definitely tenacious, Chris." It was Lynne who said it. "You don't let up on things until they're right. It's one of the things I love about you."

She paused, and Chris smiled and nodded to acknowledge the compliment.

Until she continued. "And one of the things that drives me crazy. You and those stupid expense reports."

Everyone laughed, including Chris.

TAKING STOCK

Chris put down his pen and went to the table to get a bite of his burrito.

"I think Chris has earned a five-minute break to get some food," Amy announced.

And that's when we heard a knock at the door.

Before anyone could say "come in," the door was opening and in walked Anna with a large plastic container that we all knew was filled with oatmeal chocolate chip cookies.

The room erupted in warm greetings, mostly because they loved Anna. But the thought of her cookies did nothing to dampen their enthusiasm. My wife was famous for them, and she refused to make any other kind. The last time I suggested she make a batch of plain oatmeal, she looked at me like I was deranged.

"I thought I'd come by and give you some sugar," she declared, bringing the container to the table. After a few hugs and waves and pleasantries with the team, she asked the sixty-four-thousand-dollar question.

"What are you guys doing?" She was staring at the whiteboard.

Everyone looked at one another as if to say, *you tell her*, and then started laughing.

Amy spoke first. "Where do you want us to start?"

Anna held up her hand. "Oh, I don't want to interrupt or slow you guys down. I was just curious."

Jasper interrupted. "It's not that you're slowing us down. It's just hard to explain. And we're just figuring it out ourselves."

Anna nodded and kept looking at the board.

"But," Jasper went on, "we think we figured out why your husband is so pissy."

Anna turned abruptly toward Jasper and the rest of the team and sat down at the table. "Well, I'm all ears then. I'd be glad to interrupt."

I protested jokingly. "This isn't fair."

"You're right," Anna teased back at me. "It isn't fair that I wasn't here for the whole conversation."

Everyone agreed with her.

"Okay," I announced. "Let's have someone besides me give Anna an overview of all this. She deserves that. After all, she brought us cookies."

The truth is, Anna studied psychology and theology in college, and this was right up her alley. I was confident she would enjoy the rest of our conversation and add something to it that we had missed.

Chris called the question. "Who's going to volunteer to present this? I need to eat."

Jasper raised his hand. "Since I'm good at enabling, I guess I'll do it."

Lynne stood up. "I'll help, too."

And they went to the whiteboard together.

RE-PRESENTATION

Before you start," Anna inquired, "can I ask you a question?"

"You can ask two questions if you like," Jasper responded with his customary humor.

"Is the purpose of this meeting just to figure out why Bull has been so difficult lately? Has it been that bad for you guys?"

Jasper frowned in a sad kind of way. "It's been horrible, Anna. Just horrible."

Everyone laughed.

Amy explained. "Bull's been fine, Anna. But he and I were trying to figure out why he gets stressed out so quickly, and that's where all this came from. But it's a lot more than that."

Anna seemed relieved.

Jasper wasn't finished. "But you should probably know, Anna." He paused. "Most of this is about you."

For a nanosecond, Anna seemed worried.

"Stop that, Jasper. It's mean!" Quinn yelled at her colleague while trying unsuccessfully to hold back a smile.

She turned toward Anna. "It has nothing to do with you."

Anna threw a cookie at Jasper, who caught it and put it in his mouth.

Lynne took over. "Basically, what we've figured out here is that there are six different kinds of work that someone has to do in order for us to get anything done." She pointed toward the six circles on the whiteboard. "And no one is great at all of them, which means most people are pretty bad at some of those things."

Anna was following. "And why exactly does Bull get so pissy?"

"Hey," I protested again. "I'm not pissy." I thought about it. "I'm just ill-tempered."

Anna laughed. "I'm sorry, dear."

Lynne went on. "Well, this will make sense in a few minutes. Basically, he's been spending a lot of his time doing something that he doesn't like to do, but that none of us wanted to do, either."

"Okay, I'll be patient. Go on."

Jasper had not quite finished his cookie but jumped in with his mouth full.

"The first kind of work is called *Wonder*, which is all about thinking and pondering and contemplating things. And asking questions."

"What kind of questions?" Anna asked.

Jasper swallowed. "Things like, 'Is there a better way?' or 'Is something wrong here?' or 'Are we fulfilling our full potential?'"

"That's me," Anna announced.

Amy jumped in. "It's one of my geniuses, too."

"Geniuses?" Anna wondered out loud.

"Yeah," I explained. "Jasper came up with that. We all have different areas of genius."

"Oh, I like this," Anna declared. "Keep going. I'll try not to interrupt."

I loved watching Anna interact with my colleagues. So, I went over to her, knelt down in front of her, and told her how much she meant to me. Then I kissed her.

No, I didn't. But I did think about how glad I was that she was my wife.

Jasper kept going. "The person with the Genius of Wonder asks the question or identifies the big issue, which brings us to the second Working Genius: *Invention*."

"This sounds like one of Bull's geniuses," Anna declared.

"Bingo." Jasper nodded. "Coming up with something novel or new. An idea or a product or a company. People with Invention can do this all day."

Anna looked at me. "That is so you."

I nodded. "That's one of my favorite things to do, even when it's not necessary."

She laughed. "That's what makes it a genius, I guess."

"Exactly," declared Jasper. "It gives us energy. We can't help it."

"Okay, keep going," Anna urged us excitedly.

Lynne picked up now. "The next one, after Invention, is what we've decided to call *Discernment*. It's the genius of having great instincts and intuition and judgment. These people have great gut feel about which ideas or plans are good ones, which need more work, and which are probably not so good."

"Does that mean they're experts?" Anna asked.

I jumped in. "No, that's different. These are people who just have good judgment, even around things that they don't know much about. They don't necessarily think in a linear way or use specific data. They just see patterns or—"

Anna interrupted me. "Got it." She looked around the room and settled on Lynne. "You have the Genius of Discernment, don't you?"

Lynne's eyes went wide. "Wow. You're good."

"Unfortunately, Anna doesn't have Discernment," Jasper stated matter-of-factly.

"What makes you say that?" I asked him, just a little defensively.

"Well, she married you," Jasper went on. "But you have Discernment, Bull, because you married her."

Anna tossed Jasper another cookie, and he caught it in his mouth.

"Okay, what's next?" she asked.

"With his mouth full of cookie again, Jasper managed to say, "Next, we find out why your husband has been such a pain in the ass."

WARP SPEED

Anna looked at her watch. "Can you do it in ten minutes? I have to pick up Matthew for a doctor's appointment."

Jasper began. "Here we go. The next genius is called *Galvanizing*, and it's all about rallying the troops, getting people excited, exhorting them to keep going."

Anna looked at me as though she were trying to read my mind. "You're good at that," she said hesitantly. "Aren't you?"

I nodded. "If you mean, 'Can I do it?', the answer is yes. If you mean, 'Do I like doing it all the time?', the answer is no."

"But you're always the one hounding people to get ready for church, or to get the chores done, or to finish their homework."

I nodded. "And I'm so tired of having to do that. I've never liked it, but I've just gotten used to having to do it over the years. The truth is, I feel like I have to be a jerk all the time, trying to get people to get moving."

Anna's eyes bulged out as if she had just seen something shocking. "Oh. My. Goodness."

Everyone was confused about her sudden change in attitude.

"What?" I asked her.

She explained her epiphany. "That's why you hate vacations with the Derbys. And Sunday mornings. And Cub Scouts."

I was so glad that she seemed to be understanding it.

"Who are the Derbys?" Chris wanted to know.

I answered. "They're old family friends who travel with us every year or so. We've been all over the country with them. Wonderful people."

Anna explained. "But none of them likes to rally people to do anything. And since I don't either, Bull is always having to say, 'Let's go hiking or whale watching or golfing,' and he gets grief from everyone because no one wants to do the same things."

"And that's only the half of it," I added. "Before we even go on vacation, Anna and Pam—that's Mrs. Derby—always come up with some harebrained idea, and I have to talk them out of it."

Anna seemed confused and was looking at the whiteboard. "What does that have to do with any of this?"

"It's about Discernment. I'm usually the one who says, 'Wait a minute. That wouldn't work.'"

Anna wasn't buying it, so I pushed on. "Remember when you said we should hike the Grand Canyon?"

Anna smiled in embarrassed concession and nodded her head. "Oh, yeah."

"What's wrong with hiking the Grand Canyon?" Jasper wondered out loud.

"Our kids were five and three at the time," I explained. "The Derbys had a nine-month-old."

Anna laughed. "Pam and I thought we could bring babysitters. Thank God you talked us out of it."

Chris put us back on track. "But it's the constant Galvanizing that drives him crazy. And that's why he gets so cranky."

Anna was now looking at me. "Does that explain what happened at AFS and Broadmoor?"

I nodded. "Absolutely. When I was promoted, I stopped doing what I loved and had to galvanize people all the time. I felt guilty. I resented it, which made me feel even more guilty. And eventually, I'd just lose my temper."

"And that's what's been happening here," Amy explained.

Anna suddenly seemed both sad for me and worried. "So, what are you going to do?"

Chris raised his hand. "I'm going to start doing a lot more Galvanizing, so that Bull can focus most of his time doing Invention and Discernment."

Anna frowned at me. "But you're still going to have to do some of that, I'd imagine. I mean, everyone has to do things they don't like sometimes."

"Yes, we've established that," I agreed. "And I really don't mind doing it here and there. It's just a problem when I'm constantly being pulled in that direction and having less and less time and energy to do what I'm actually good at."

"This is so interesting," Anna declared. "So, what comes next?"

Quinn took over. "Well, when someone galvanizes, someone else has to answer the call." She looked at the board. "We call that the Genius of *Enablement*."

"Jasper has this genius," Lynne explained, and then teased, "But he makes you deal with all his mean humor, so it's kind of a wash."

Anna liked Jasper. "He's not that mean."

"Yes, I am," Jasper clarified. "But I'll do anything that people need me to do."

I turned to Anna. "This has to be one of your geniuses."

"You think so?" She was genuinely unsure.

"Are you kidding? Every time you get anywhere near the school or church, you come home with a new project."

She nodded. "You're right. I can't help it. I like to help people who need it."

"And you're great at knowing what people need at home, too. It's your genius."

She relented. "I just wished I knew how to galvanize others to help me more. I usually end up having to do too much of it myself at the last minute."

"So do I," exclaimed Quinn. "I always complain that no one helps me. But I have to admit that I don't like to ask for help."

Anna looked at me and laughed. "That's what Bull always says about me."

Chris jumped in. "Okay, you've got five minutes before you have to leave, and we have one more genius to go."

"Right, let me have it."

Jasper turned to the board. "The last genius, which comes after Enablement, is what we call *Tenacity*. These are people who love to finish things. They get energy and joy and fulfillment from moving things across the finish line, even if they have to overcome obstacles to do it."

"That sounds like a galvanizer," Anna wondered.

"It's different," Jasper explained. "Tenacity is about the task itself, while Galvanizing is about rallying people. Tenacity is about staying on top of the work until it's done, on time, and up to standards."

Anna looked at me and laughed. "That's definitely not me."

"It's not me either," I added.

She laughed. "That's why neither of us likes to do the laundry or the bills or the lawn." She paused. "It's a good thing we have four kids who do chores."

"Which one does the bills?" Chris asked.

Anna smiled. "I was going to see if you wanted to take on a little part-time work at our house, Chris."

He laughed. "If you pay me in cookies, I'll consider it."

Anna checked her watch and looked at me again. "So, what are my geniuses again?" Then she looked back at the board. "How many can one person have?"

"I don't know," I answered. "This is all new. But I think I have two."

Jasper weighed in. "Me, too."

The others studied the board and agreed.

"I wish I didn't have to go. This is so fun," Anna said. "I miss having adult conversations."

As always, everyone assured her that she was welcome to come back soon.

As Anna was leaving, she stopped and turned around. Looking at the whiteboard again, she announced, "I think you should turn those circles into gears, the kind with the interlocking teeth." She interlaced her fingers to show us what she meant. "The geniuses fit together and need one another, and I think that would be a better visual."

As she walked out the door, everyone agreed that her idea made perfect sense.

"We should hire that woman," Lynne declared.

"Are you kidding?" I protested. "My life would fall apart. And besides, I don't think she likes me."

Jasper agreed, and with that, we took another break.

CONTEXT

When we returned, Amy asked the first question. "So, what does all this mean?"

"How's that for a specific question?" Jasper said.

She explained. "I mean, what are we going to do with this?"

I spoke first. "First, we're going to clarify what Chris is going to be doing as far as Galvanizing goes. We're going to shift his job to something of a Chief Operating Officer, I think."

Chris wrote something in his notebook.

"Second," I went on, "we're going to figure out how each of our jobs might need to change based on our Working Geniuses."

Quinn raised her hand but didn't wait to be called upon. "I've already figured out one area. I need to get involved in client planning a little earlier because I can evaluate our plans and make changes better than Jasper."

Jasper nodded and managed to restrain himself from making a joke.

She went on. "And I need to have him check my team's work

when we're in execution mode, because it's too easy for me to settle when we hit obstacles."

Again, Jasper agreed, prompting Chris to take further notes.

"I can't tell you how nice it is for me," I announced, "to know that Chris is capturing all this and will remind everyone what they need to do. I honestly feel liberated."

Amy jumped in now. "Hey, why don't we just try to confirm everyone's geniuses right now?"

There was unanimous consent, so Chris quickly rewrote the model using six gears on the board and put the name of each genius in them.

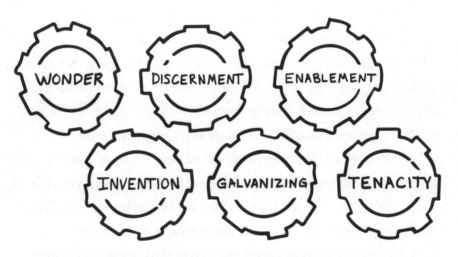

I provided some instruction. "Remember, this is about what you love doing. Try to come up with your best guess as to what gives you energy and joy, even if you're not sure."

For the next ten minutes or so, everyone stared at the board and wrote down their answers. Chris called the question.

"Okay, let's start with Bull."

"I'm pretty sure mine are Invention and Discernment."

Heads around the room nodded, and Chris wrote my name next to those gears.

We agreed, and so he pointed at Amy.

"Mine are Wonder and Discernment, I think."

Everyone considered her answer for a few seconds.

"I think you nailed it," Jasper announced. "You're always asking questions, and you have great judgment."

She seemed pleased, until he finished. "You certainly don't have Tenacity."

Everyone laughed.

"You really are mean, aren't you?" she teased.

"Hey, I admitted it."

Chris pointed at Jasper. "Okay, mean guy. What are yours?"

"Enablement and Tenacity, right?"

Amy teased him. "It's certainly not Discernment."

Jasper laughed but went on. "You know, I hate to admit it, but it's true. I don't always trust my gut. I like data. Half the time, I don't understand which body cavity Bull pulls his instincts from. But he's usually right, so I just trust him."

Chris wrote the names on the board and turned to Lynne.

"I think I need some help with this." She paused. "I can rule out Invention and Galvanizing. Those are my nightmares." She stared at the gears on the board as though the answer might appear there. "And I think I'm just okay at Tenacity and Enablement."

Quinn jumped in. "Right. So you have Discernment and Wonder."

"Remember," I added, "it's about what gives you joy and energy. And I don't know if you enjoy it, but you have fantastic judgment."

Lynne's frown disappeared. "Yeah, that's right. It's so easy for me to evaluate your ideas, Bull. I don't know where you get them, but once they're out there, I really enjoy giving you feedback and figuring out which will work best."

Amy responded first. "I totally see the Discernment in you. You don't let up until we know we're done. But the Wonder thing kind of surprises me."

Lynne laughed. "If you guys could see me at home, you'd be shocked. Dave says I get lost staring out the window. I have my head in the clouds for hours. I guess I just don't do it here."

"Wait a second," I interrupted. "Who was it that originally came up with the idea for adopting a charity last Christmas?"

Lynne responded first. "Well, it was you who found that shelter downtown."

I shook my head. "But who was the one who said we should focus on one charity so we could make a real difference?" I didn't wait for her to answer. "It was you. And you were the one who kept saying that something just didn't feel right about our printing vendor."

Chris nodded. "Yeah, you were driving me crazy by asking me over and over why we hadn't found a better printer. 'Are they really the best we can do?' How many times did you ask me that?"

Lynne held up her hand with all five fingers extended. "At least five." She smiled.

Chris laughed. "You and Amy are always making us stop to think about things before we make decisions."

"But we drive you crazy," Amy argued.

"No," I countered, "you drive Jasper crazy because he just wants to move on and get things done."

Everyone agreed.

Chris raised his hand, smiling. "They drive me crazy, too."

Lynne laughed, and challenged him. "What are your geniuses again, Chris?"

"Well, I think we've established that I love Galvanizing and Tenacity."

"Absolutely," Lynne agreed. "That's you in a nutshell."

"And what about Quinn?" Amy asked.

"She definitely has Enablement," Jasper offered.

I weighed in. "She's also a discerner."

Amy added, "You know, I go to Quinn whenever I need a second opinion about whether a project is going to work."

"I love when people ask me my opinion," Quinn admitted. "About anything, really."

Jasper laughed out loud and looked at Quinn. "I'm twice your age and have a lot more experience in advertising than you do, and yet I ask you what you think about everything. Before I send something to a client, I show it to you. Before I decide on a media partner, I ask you. Hell, I even ask you what to get my wife for her birthday."

"*That* is Discernment," I confirmed. "And we all agree that Quinn has it."

Chris wrote Quinn's name on the board, and the team's picture was complete. A few things jumped out right away.

LOW-HANGING FRUIT

dove in first. "Well, this certainly explains things."

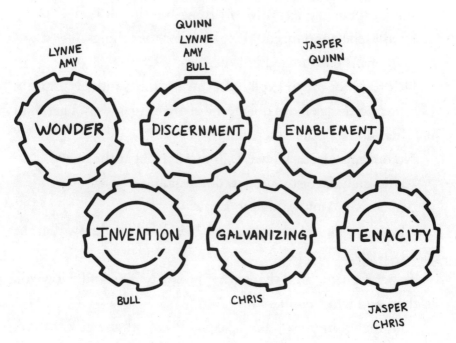

"We have multiple people who love Wonder, Discernment, Enablement, and Tenacity, and only one in Invention and Galvanizing."

"What does that mean?" Lynne asked out loud to no one in particular.

Quinn answered before I could. "It means we really need Chris to do most of the Galvanizing so Bull can focus on Invention."

Amy was nodding her agreement but was also frowning.

"What's wrong?" I asked her.

"Well, I think what Quinn said is exactly right, but I have a feeling that we're missing something here."

"Tell me more," I prodded her.

"I don't know. It's just . . ." She paused. "I don't know."

We sat there and let Amy sort things out in her brain.

Finally, she announced, "It's the other four things."

"Go on," I encouraged her.

"It's hard for me to explain," Amy said, hesitating. "I mean, if I have two things I love doing, those are my geniuses. I get that. But what do I call the other things?"

No one answered. We were all just staring at the board.

"This is my favorite thing to do," I said.

"What is?" Amy wanted to know.

"Trying to figure out new things like this. I just know that the answer is about to emerge."

Jasper replied, "And that's what I don't understand. How you do that, and why you like it."

And then it hit me. "Okay, Jasper. Play with me here. I think I have an idea. Tell me how much you hate Invention."

"I was just joking." He seemed slightly apologetic.

"No, I'm serious. How much do you hate inventing? Or, for that matter, any of the other skills that aren't your genius?"

Jasper had to think about it. "Well," he said, looking at the whiteboard, "I can Wonder sometimes. You know, I've been known to ponder and contemplate from time to time, usually with a beer in my hand."

We laughed.

He went on. "And though I'm not a discerner, and I need Quinn to tell me what to get my wife for her birthday, I do have *some* intuition about what a client might need. So, I don't hate that." He paused. "But I can say that I really, really hate Galvanizing people and making them do things they don't already want to do. I'd rather just do it myself."

"What about Invention?" Amy wanted to know.

"Well, I get sick to my stomach when someone asks me to come up with something new without any guidelines or structure. I really, really hate it."

I turned to Amy. "What about you?"

"Do I hate inventing?"

"No, tell me how you feel about the four things that aren't your genius."

"Got it," she said. "Let's see. I'm not an inventor, but I could do that in a pinch if I had to. But I wouldn't be able to do it like Bull."

She paused while she studied the board. "And I don't mind when I have to enable others from time to time. Again, not my favorite thing, but not something I dread."

She took a breath. "I said earlier that I really hate Galvanizing people. Drains me of my energy. And as much as I hate to admit it, Jasper was right about my Tenacity. I get no energy from finishing things. After the initial stage of a project, I lose interest and want to move on to the next one."

Chris winced. "I don't want to insult you, or other people who don't have Tenacity, Amy." He hesitated. "But that kind of sounds like laziness."

"Bam!" Jasper shouted. "Chris just called Amy lazy."

We all cracked up. Except Chris.

"That's not what I was saying," he protested apologetically. "I was saying it might sound—"

Amy interrupted him. "I know what you meant. I didn't take it that way." She thought about it some more. "But I don't think I'm lazy."

"Even I know you're not lazy," Jasper announced, "as much as I'd like to say you are."

Something occurred to me. "You know, I've always felt guilty for not liking to finish things. And, yeah, I feel lazy sometimes because of it. But I think it's just one of the things that drains me of my energy the most."

"And you're definitely not lazy," Lynne affirmed. "But should you get a free pass on finishing things, on Tenacity, just because you don't like doing it?"

Everyone seemed to be looking for me to answer. "No way," I declared in agreement. "Everyone has to do things they don't like. But if we put someone in a job that requires them to do a lot of what they hate doing, we're not being smart."

"What about the things they don't hate, but they don't love?" she wanted to know.

"I think that's different. In fact, we should probably distinguish between the other four activities. If what we love and are naturally good at are our geniuses, what would we call the things we hate?"

"Miseries," Amy offered.

Chris wrote it on the whiteboard, and we all considered it.

I frowned. "I like the word *frustration* better than *misery*. I don't know why."

We all sat there staring at the whiteboard, waiting for an answer to emerge.

Amy broke the silence. "Yeah, it's really about frustration. It's draining more than it's miserable. It's frustrating."

Jasper chimed in. "Let's not wordsmith this to death. Frustration is good."

Chris erased *miseries* and wrote *frustrations*.

"And what about the middle category?" I pushed. "Not your genius but not your frustration."

"Competency," Quinn suggested. "You can do it pretty well for a while, even if you don't like it."

Everyone seemed to like that idea.

"And there it is," I declared. "Six categories of genius. Each of us will have a couple geniuses, a couple competencies, and a couple frustrations."

We all just sat and stared at the board as though we were looking for something else, or perhaps, for something wrong. No one said a word for almost a full minute.

Chris broke the silence. "I think we should play with this for a few weeks and see what we learn."

We agreed, and just like that, we left the room with a strange mix of exhaustion and anticipation. I was so excited I couldn't contain myself.

IMPLEMENTATION

When I went home that evening, Anna had already begun putting her insights into practice. She had rolled the whiteboard from my little office into the family room and drawn the six gears on it.

Before she even said hello to me, she dove in. "So, if my geniuses are Wonder and Enablement, and yours are Invention and Discernment, then we're pretty much screwed around here."

I laughed. "Wow. You're starting to sound like Jasper."

"I'm sorry." She smiled slightly and came over and kissed me. "I'm seriously just really amped up here, and more than a little concerned."

I put my backpack down—which my kids tease me about because I carry it over my shoulder instead of on my back—and went to the whiteboard. I scanned it for a moment.

I realized that I hadn't explained to her our insights around working competencies and frustrations, so I spent the next ten minutes doing just that. Anna's mind started racing.

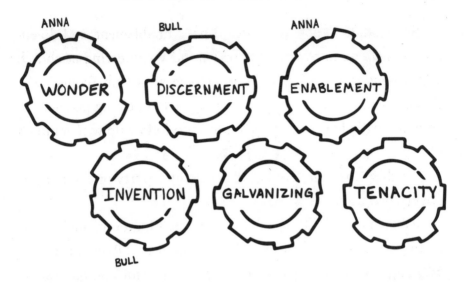

"Let's see." I said. "Neither of us has Galvanizing or Tenacity as geniuses, but Galvanizing is one of my competencies. But both of us have Tenacity as frustrations, and that is our problem."

"Exactly. Neither of us likes to finish things or wrestle with details," Anna declared.

"Ouch," I said. "That explains a lot."

"Ouch is right. The late fees on bills. The kids being late to school. The budget that we blow through because we don't track our spending."

Something suddenly dawned on me. "Oh crap. This is bad."

"What?"

"I just realized that most of the Tenacity stuff around here falls on you. Here I am complaining about having to galvanize, but at least that's one of my competencies. You hate details and deadlines and execution as much as I do, but so much of what you have to do every day is all about that." I felt really bad for her, and that I hadn't realized this years earlier.

She studied the board. "Well, I have Enablement, so I do enjoy the helping part. I really don't mind volunteering at church and driving the kids around and helping with Cub Scouts." She thought about it some more. "As long as I'm helping people, I'm actually really happy. But when I have to follow up with a bunch of detail work, I lose interest."

"Is that why you don't mind throwing a party or cooking for twenty people at Christmas—"

Anna interrupted me. "But I hate cooking every night, and cleaning up is my nightmare." She laughed. "Remember that Thanksgiving when we left dishes in the sink for two days?"

"That was my bad," I acknowledged. "And remember how devastated your dad was when he came by and saw the kitchen?"

"I thought he was going to disown me. He definitely has Tenacity."

"What about the garage?" I suddenly realized. "Every time he goes in there, he shakes his head like we're a disgrace."

"So, what are we going to do?" Anna asked.

"We'll just keep him out of the garage when he visits," I responded matter-of-factly.

"That's not what I mean, you knucklehead. What are we going to do about our lack of Tenacity? It's not going to get any easier."

"Well . . ." I thought about it for a second. "First, we're not going to feel like we're terrible, lazy people anymore; it's just not our genius."

"That's helpful," she acknowledged. "But what about the work itself?"

"Maybe we should find a way to outsource more of it."

"Like hire a butler?" She laughed.

"Let's get that robot from the Jetsons. What was her name?"

"Rosie," Anna remembered. "Yes, we need Rosie the Robot."

"Or maybe we find a way to pay for someone to come in and do some household stuff, and some administrative stuff, a couple times a week."

"Administrative stuff?" Anna wondered out loud. "I don't know about that."

"We could find a college student, even someone we know, who wouldn't mind paying some bills and running errands, or doing laundry," I suggested. "Heck, that would be a sweet gig for someone who wants to make some extra money."

"How soon can this person start?" Anna joked. "And can they call me every morning and remind me what's on my schedule?"

And then something dawned on me. "Oh crap."

"What?"

"My schedule. I just remembered that I have a meeting at church tonight."

"What kind of meeting?" she asked.

"The International Festival planning committee that you volunteered me for," I explained, rolling my eyes.

She winced. "I'm sorry. It's hard for me to say no, and you said you'd like to get more involved."

"See, that's Enablement. You don't like to say no. That's not so hard for me."

"Do you think you can get out of it?"

"No. I did say that I need to be more involved. I need to pull my weight, in terms of service hours. I'll go."

"What time does it start?"

I checked my watch. "Five minutes ago."

"That's okay," Anna reassured me. "Nothing ever starts on time over there besides Mass."

So, I left.

COMMITTEE

True to Anna's promise, when I arrived twelve minutes later, I was not the only one going into the conference room at St. Matthew's parish.

There were seven people there, including me and Father John, the pastor, who was just a few years older than me.

"Let's get started, everyone," the pastor announced. "I'd like to get you out of here at a decent hour."

Everyone sat down, and Fr. John led us in prayer.

Then an older guy, whom I didn't know but recognized from Mass, went to the front of the room and began.

"Thank you all for coming tonight. I'm Finn Collins, and I've been running the International Festival for the past seven years, since Bob and Peggy Carlson retired. As you may know, we've had fewer and fewer people attend the festival for the past couple of years, and we actually lost money on the event last year. So, I'm hoping that we can bounce back this fall and even make something of a profit."

I interrupted. "Excuse me, Finn, but hope is not a strategy."

Now, I didn't actually say that, as tame as it may sound. At parish meetings, I learned the hard way that people were often offended by direct language and blunt observations. Besides, that would have been obnoxious. So, I said nothing.

Finn continued. "Okay, let's divide up responsibilities so that we can start making progress. We have three months exactly until the day of the festival, and if I've learned anything over the past seven years, we're going to need all that time to get ready."

Finn started handing out papers of some kind that I assumed had something to do with the different roles that we would be signing up to do. And then I heard a gentle voice behind me ask a wonderful question.

"Can we talk about the purpose of the International Festival?"

Along with three other guys in my row, I turned to see a shortish woman sitting in the back of the room. Somehow, I hadn't noticed her, or the sleeping toddler in her arms, when I arrived.

Finn looked confused. "Well . . ." He looked at Fr. John. "The International Festival is one of the parish activities we have every year."

I thought he was going to keep explaining, and I think others did, too, because we were all quietly waiting, but the man just stopped right there.

The woman with the toddler tried again. "Yes, I know. But why do we do it every year?" She didn't wait for a response. "Is it worth all the planning and preparation? Could it be different, or better?"

The room was silent. Finn looked at Fr. John, who looked at someone else in the front row. As fair and relatively innocuous as her comment was, there was a palpable sense of tension in the room. You'd have thought good ol' Finn had ripped a fart.

And that's when I decided that I should jump in, for real this time. "I think that's a fair question. It's always a good idea to review things from time to time to make sure they're still relevant."

For just a moment, Finn shot me a glance that made me think he was going to leap over the first row of folding chairs and strangle me. Thankfully, he didn't. But I'm pretty sure I could have taken him on if he did. Finn wasn't in the best of shape.

A woman sitting next to Fr. John spoke next. "I don't think it's a good use of our time to question the purpose of something we've been doing for twenty-five years."

And that's when I remembered the Working Genius model. The shortish lady with the toddler wasn't being difficult; she was simply wondering. And it was up to me to save her, even if I had to take on Mrs. Church Lady to do it.

"Hold on a second, everyone." I looked back at the toddler-toting woman behind me. "I think the question you're asking is a good one, and an important one. And I don't think we should take it as a criticism at all."

The room was suddenly quieter than it had been before, if that's possible.

I continued. "Before we do any activities at the parish, other than the Sacraments, of course, we should always be asking ourselves if that activity is worthwhile and achieving its goals. I'm guessing that we don't stop doing things very often because we're afraid that someone might be upset."

At first, no one spoke. Then Fr. John shouted, "Are you kidding?! I've been feeling that way for years! Putting a program or a ministry or an activity out of its misery is something that I feel I'm not allowed to do, and so we end up having a thousand different things, and none of them has the resources and time required to make them really good."

I half expected Mrs. Church Lady and Finn to throw a fit, but something amazing happened. They seemed relieved.

Finn jumped in now. "Don't get me wrong, people. I'd be fine if we stepped back from all this and reevaluated it all." He smiled. "I just figured that it was sacred, and that everyone would have a cow."

We laughed at the play on words, along with Finn, who I'm not sure intended to be funny.

He went on. "When I was running Tahoe Builders, we did semi-annual reviews of our work with the goal of killing any projects that were preventing us from doing other, more important ones."

Had I heard that correctly? Good ol' Finn Collins, the sleepy-looking church volunteer, ran the largest construction firm in the Reno-Tahoe area? Shame on me. I had sold him short.

Mrs. Church Lady jumped in. "Well, when I was the head of American Airlines, we did the same thing." I kid you not. That's what she really said.

Of course, she was teasing Finn, and everyone, including me, eventually howled. As it turned out, she had a better sense of humor than I'd thought. I decided that I needed to stop judging people.

Now, surging with a combination of guilt and lack of self-control, I raised my hand and spoke. "My name is Bull Brooks, and I'd like to suggest—"

The shortish woman interrupted me. "Oh, you're Anna's husband," she declared excitedly.

Mrs. Church Lady, who introduced herself as Betty, exclaimed, "I love your wife. She's the best volunteer we have."

My guilt was replaced with pride in my bride, and I went on. "I'll pass that on to Anna. Thank you." I paused. "So, I'd like to volunteer to facilitate a quick discussion around this, if that's okay. I did this in my advertising agency, and I think I can help."

"That would be great," Finn declared earnestly, and used his hands to sort of invite me to the front of the room, where, thankfully, there was a whiteboard.

CHURCH GENIUS

Suddenly, I was a little nervous. I mean, I didn't want to let my famous and beloved wife down by looking like a doofus in front of these people.

Buying time, I picked up a marker and went to the board.

"Okay, before we talk about the purpose of the festival, let me show you something that we've figured out at work."

I drew the six circles, deciding I didn't have the time to make them look like gears.

"When it comes to work, whether it's running a school, raising money for the new family center, or organizing a festival, there are six different steps involved."

I wrote the word *Wonder* in the first circle. "What you were doing a few minutes ago." I pointed at the woman with the toddler.

"I'm Terri," she told me, smiling.

"Hi, Terri. This is what you were doing when you asked the question 'Why do we have the festival?'"

I turned to the others. "She was wondering, pondering, contemplating, asking the big question. And that is the first step in any endeavor."

Fr. John laughed. "That's what Mrs. Lorenzo did that prompted us to build the family center. She came to me and said, 'There must be a better way for us to help moms with kids who come to the parish to volunteer or do Bible study or go to Confession.' I'll always remember that day, and Mrs. Lorenzo."

"I'm guessing that Terri does that in other areas of her life, too," I said, essentially asking Terri to confirm or deny my guess.

She laughed as though I had said something insightful. "I do it all the time. It drives my husband crazy."

I went on. "So, Wonder is probably one of your geniuses."

"Geniuses?" Finn asked.

"A genius is a God-given talent, a natural gift that gives you energy and joy and that you're usually good at doing."

Fr. John smiled and nodded. "Got it. Yes, Mrs. Lorenzo was a genius at wondering."

"So, what happened next, after she asked that question?" I asked.

"Well," the priest responded, "I thought about it for a while, I guess."

"But how did the family center come about?" I persisted.

"Well..." The priest frowned as he tried to remember. "I think Jack Martinez came up with the idea to build a structure that had classrooms, restrooms, day care, and a media center all in one."

"That's the second step in work," I explained as I wrote it in the circle. "Invention. Someone has to come up with a solution, a new idea, a proposal. Some people have that genius."

People were now starting to take notes, which I thought was pretty cool. So I went on and explained Discernment, Galvanizing, Enablement and Tenacity. It took ten minutes, and every single one of them seemed to get it! I couldn't believe it.

Now that I had all six circles on the board, I brought us back to the festival.

"So, let's start with Wonder. What is the purpose of the festival? How could it be better?"

Fr. John went first. "I'd like to make it more connected to our faith. And to helping others. No offense, Finn."

"None taken, Father. I'm pretty sure I don't have any of this Wonder or Invention stuff. I'm a Tenacity guy, so if you give me direction, I'll make it happen."

Fr. John seemed relieved. "So, how can we make it more faith-filled, more charitable, more passionate?"

I raised my hand, which was awkward given that I was standing in the front of the room. "I have an idea."

"Is Invention your genius?" Betty asked kindly.

"In fact, it is," I admitted, as humbly as I could. "I can't help but think of new ideas, even when I shouldn't."

She laughed. "Well, we need you to do some inventing now."

I smiled. "So, here's what I'm thinking. What if we had each of the different nationality groups organize their food and other cultural things around a saint from their country?"

Fr. John sat up in his chair and smiled. "I like this."

I went on. "And what if, instead of the adults putting on the festival for our kids, we actually got our students involved in putting on the festival, but for families from really poor schools out in the valley? Serve them food, do the games and the face painting, and all that stuff."

I paused, and something occurred to me. "Everyone always says they want their kids to do mission trips, but they don't want to travel to foreign countries. Well, there are plenty of people in need within driving distance, and we can make this an outreach program."

"Well," Finn declared, "we're already losing money, so we don't have to worry about that."

Everyone laughed.

One of the other men in the room announced, "Hey, if we make this an outreach program, I can get donations to cover the costs. I don't like to ask people to donate for a carnival, but if it's a way to serve the poor, I know plenty of businesses that will help. I'm pretty sure we could break even, which would be better than last year."

Betty declared, "This sounds wonderful!"

For the next thirty minutes, we brainstormed. People even rejected a few ideas, including the one where I suggested we have Fr. John sit in a dunking booth filled with horchata. No, I didn't suggest that, but when I got home, I convinced Anna that I did just so I could see the look on her face.

By the end of the night, we had the outlines of a plan. Fr. John announced that he and Betty were galvanizers, and with Finn's Tenacity, I was pretty sure that the International Festival was getting a new lease on life, and that I was a wonderful guy for making it happen.

Again, kidding.

REALITY

This is the part of the story where I go back to work the next day with great expectations for relief and excitement about my job and about the roles that everyone else would play. It's where I get disappointed because we slide back into our old grooves and forget about what we talked about the day before and nothing really changes. You know, three steps forward, two and a half steps back.

But it didn't happen. I mean, we didn't all come skipping into the office like the seven dwarfs, minus Grumpy, of course. But everyone, and I mean everyone, was still talking about their geniuses. And their frustrations.

And everyone had gone home and discussed it with their spouses or friends, and had hilarious and meaningful stories to tell. Something was going on.

And best of all was Chris. He came to work before anyone else, announced to the executive team that we would be meeting as soon as everyone arrived, and then brought us into the conference room.

He looked at me. "Okay, Bull, I decided that I was going to take what you said yesterday seriously. So I'm going to take a stab at Galvanizing here."

No one said anything at first, and I could tell that Chris was a little shaky about our lack of response.

So, being the smart-ass that I am, I said, "Don't you think that you should have come to me privately to talk about this first?"

Though it was only a second and a half, the look on Chris's face made me regret my stunt. I explained immediately, "I'm joking. I'm joking. I'm just joking."

Jasper thought it was hilarious. No one else did, at least not until Chris realized that there was absolutely no seriousness to what I was saying.

Note to self: Choose jokes more carefully. Use your Discernment.

I went on. "In fact, if you're going to galvanize, this is exactly what I want you to do. Push. Take risks. Make us a little uncomfortable."

For the next hour, we reviewed our current clients, discussed our best new client opportunities, and laid out the priorities for the rest of the month. It was fantastic. I was still the CEO, but I didn't have to ask all the questions and push people for clarity.

Chris seemed more engaged than I had ever seen him.

In the course of our discussion, we shifted some of Quinn's job to focus more on helping me manage people's personal development. Her combination of Enablement and Discernment made that a perfect role for her, regardless of what we thought her job was thirty-six hours earlier.

After the meeting, I spent the next four hours focused exclusively on ideas. Amy and I talked about potential clients to target. Lynne and I brainstormed about digital ads and messaging to pitch to the resort. And Jasper asked me to review the work that he and his team had been doing for one of our oldest clients.

It was the best four hours I had spent at work in months. And according to Amy, Lynne, and Jasper and his team, it was really productive for them, too.

Later in the afternoon, I worked with Chris, Quinn, and Amy to put together something of a structure for how we would go about organizing, staffing, and evaluating the success of our projects. I should clarify here that this wasn't the first time I had thought of any of this. I wasn't a cretin. It was just that having people around me who were better than I was at this part of my job, and who enjoyed it, made it so much more effective.

It wasn't until I went home that night that I realized how much had changed in one day. It was Anna who noticed it first.

DEBRIEF

She was in the kitchen helping one of our kids make quesadillas. The fans were blowing and the windows were open to prevent the smoke alarms from going off; evidently, the first batch had burned.

Even in the midst of what could have been a storm, my wife seemed excited to see me.

"Why didn't you tell me what happened at church last night?" she asked as she waved a dish towel to disperse the light smoke.

"You were asleep, and I didn't want to wake you up," I defended myself.

"So, what happened?" She had a grin on her face.

"It sounds like you already know. What did you hear?"

Putting down the dish towel, she explained, "Well, Betty said you helped them redesign the festival, or something like that. And she said you were funny."

"Well, that's my goal. To be funny."

"You know what I mean. She said you were really helpful. What did you do?"

I sat down at the kitchen table, below the layer of smoke, and explained to her how I had used the Working Genius to help them sort out the conversation they were having. I told her how I had underestimated some of the people at the meeting. And how they had lifted me on their shoulders and carried me out of the room at the end of the meeting.

She swatted me with the towel.

And then she asked the big question. "So, how was work?"

I took a deep breath, gave it a few moments of thought, and responded casually, "I think it was the best day I've had in years."

"Whoa." Her eyes went wide. "That's a change. Tell me more."

I told her about Chris and the morning meeting. And about giving Quinn new responsibilities.

"How are they feeling about all this?" she asked.

"I can't be sure, but I honestly think they're thrilled." And then I told her about the afternoon.

Fun. Fun. Fun.

"And I haven't enjoyed a day at work this much in years."

Anna was genuinely surprised. "And you really think it's because of what you did yesterday?"

"I do. But it's just one day."

VIRAL

The following day, Quinn came to my office—which was more of a conference room than an office—with an idea.

"Is it all right if I take the littles through the genius thing today?"

The littles were the young people who worked in the agency. They came up with the name themselves, if you're wondering. They included Shane, Makena, Max, Kristen, and Kirstin.

The hardest-working little was Kristen. Her only flaw was that people often confused her with Kirstin because of their names. I probably should have fired Kirstin just to avoid that confusion, but I didn't. That's how kind I am. In truth, the littles were great kids, even if their performance levels varied.

"On one condition," I said to Quinn. "That you let me do it with you."

Thankfully, she was glad to have me on board. But she had a condition for me, too.

"You need to know that we're still having problems with Max. I've talked to him about the detail issues and the follow-through a half dozen times. He also seems genuinely committed to getting better. And then it happens again. I don't know if he's going to make it."

My heart sank a little. I really liked the littles, and was rooting for Max. He was genuinely humble, enthusiastic about our business, and seemed to work hard.

"If he isn't cutting it, then maybe this isn't the right place for him," I said. "But it's a shame because he seemed to be such a good fit when we hired him."

Quinn nodded, in a slightly dejected sort of way. "I know. I thought the same thing. But the mistakes he's making are driving me crazy."

I assured Quinn that I trusted her judgment, and told her I would see her later in the day at the session.

We had pizza delivered, and decided to invite Jasper to come along for comic relief. We had no idea how important, and serious, his participation would be.

RESCUE

Quinn and I took turns explaining the six categories to the littles, and we were both relieved that they seemed as genuinely interested in the concepts as they were capable of quickly grasping it all.

It took a while for everyone to settle on the geniuses that applied to them, but eventually the picture became clear.

Shane's geniuses were Galvanizing and Enablement, Makena's were Galvanizing and Tenacity, Max's were Invention and Discernment, and wouldn't you know it, Kristen and Kirstin both had Enablement and Tenacity as their geniuses. Frankly, my head was swimming trying to keep it all straight, until Jasper went to the board and wrote it in a new way.

He not only listed everyone's name next to the genius categories but he also listed their frustrations.

Before we could even think of what it might mean, the littles were diving in.

"Three of us have Tenacity," Shane announced. "All the women."

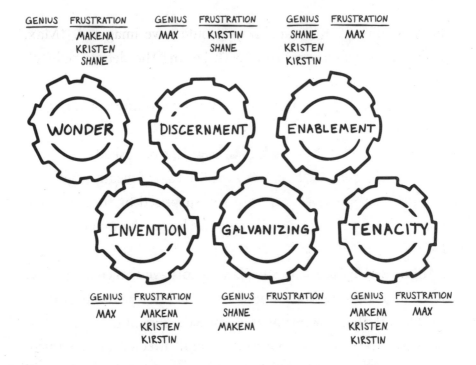

GENIUS	FRUSTRATION		GENIUS	FRUSTRATION		GENIUS	FRUSTRATION
MAKENA			MAX	KIRSTIN		SHANE	MAX
KRISTEN				SHANE		KRISTEN	
SHANE						KIRSTIN	

WONDER   DISCERNMENT   ENABLEMENT

INVENTION   GALVANIZING   TENACITY

GENIUS	FRUSTRATION		GENIUS	FRUSTRATION		GENIUS	FRUSTRATION
MAX	MAKENA		SHANE			MAKENA	MAX
	KRISTEN		MAKENA			KRISTEN	
	KIRSTIN					KIRSTIN	

Makena teased, "Yeah, we're tired of cleaning up after you boys."

Everyone laughed.

Jasper interrupted. "Wait a second." He got their attention. "And you have Tenacity as one of your competencies, your middle areas." He directed the comment at Shane.

"Why does that matter?" Shane asked.

"Well, there is only one person who has their name in red next to *Tenacity*." Jasper paused. "And that's Max."

The room was suddenly more silent than it should have been. I looked at Max and could tell he was uncomfortable.

Before Quinn or I could say anything, Jasper went on, and in the most direct but elegant way I could have imagined. "Max, you've been having problems with getting the details right on some of your stuff, correct?"

If there was any doubt about Max's discomfort, it was gone now. "Uh, yeah. I have."

"And how does that make you feel?" Jasper asked.

Max hesitated. "Uh, pretty awful, I'd say. I mean, when—"

Jasper interrupted him. "Are you surprised by that? I mean, do you think Bull would be doing any better than you are if he had to do what you do?"

Max looked at me. I smiled and shrugged, trying to make him feel okay about the question.

"Well, I don't know," Max admitted.

Now I entered the conversation and directed my comment at Jasper. "Do you remember our first year at the agency? How many times did you save my butt because I left something important out of a presentation?"

"You were a nightmare," Jasper agreed. "Just like Max."

Max actually laughed, which was a relief to everyone in the room.

"So, what was your problem?" Jasper asked me.

I smiled. "I was terrible at some parts of the job, but so were you if I remember correctly."

"I certainly was." Jasper was not in the slightest bit being sarcastic. "If I had to come up with new ideas or give a client feedback in the middle of a presentation, I'd poop my pants."

Everyone laughed.

"No, I'm serious," Jasper corrected them. "I was terrible at those things." And then he corrected himself. "But I didn't actually poop my pants."

After the room stopped laughing, he went on. "So, the way I see it, the agency could have done one of two things. They could have gotten rid of both of us because neither of us was good at every aspect of our work." He paused for effect. "Or they could have kept us working together so we could complement one another. Thankfully, they chose the latter because otherwise we wouldn't be here today."

Now Quinn dove in. "Who have you been working with on most of your projects lately, Max?"

He looked around the room. "Shane and Amy," he finally responded.

I stood up like a lawyer about to make a point to the jury. "And neither of them has the Genius of Tenacity, right?"

Quinn nodded.

"So you're pretty screwed then, am I right?" I asked Max rhetorically.

"You're definitely screwed," Jasper announced.

Everyone laughed.

"But just because no one on the team has Tenacity doesn't mean it's okay to make careless mistakes," Quinn offered. The words sound harsh, I know, but she said it very nicely.

"It's not an excuse," I agreed, "but it's an important explanation. And it's fair to say that when we put that team together, we probably could have anticipated what would happen."

Quinn seemed just a little confused.

"I mean," I added, "if we had known about their Working Genius profiles."

Then Max asked the most important question, one that took some guts. "So, what am I supposed to do? I'm never going to be as good at the details as Makena, Kirstin, and Kristen, and probably not even as good as Shane. Maybe I'm not cut out for this."

There was a moment of stunned silence at the bold statement.

Jasper surprised me by what he said next. "Here's how I see it, and I hate to admit it, but I learned it from Bull." He turned toward Max. "If you're a cultural fit, then you belong. If not, we should probably make you available to the market."

Silence again, until Jasper continued.

"And I can say with confidence that you're a cultural fit. We just have you in the wrong role, and that's our fault."

"What role should he be in?" asked Makena.

"I don't know," Jasper admitted, "but not one that is all about detail and follow-through." He seemed finished, but then went on. "Hey, if we put Bull in that role, he'd fail. I know. I was the one who saved his butt when he was your age."

Max nodded reluctantly. "I guess not." He paused and then continued. "But what if we don't have a role that fits my needs?"

Another bold statement. I was liking Max more and more.

"That's possible," I acknowledged, "but it's not something we should be thinking about right now."

"Then, what should we be thinking about?" Quinn asked.

"We should be figuring out how we're using everyone on this team. I'm guessing that some of Max's skills might be useful to someone else."

"How do you go about that?" Max wanted to know.

"I don't know," I said. "But I bet we could figure it out in twenty minutes."

People seemed confused.

And then Jasper said, "My money is on Bull. I've seen him do this before."

DIAGNOSIS

I started by focusing on everyone's working frustrations, their lower two areas of skill.

"Okay, three of you have Invention and Wonder as one of your areas of frustration."

I circled those words on the board. Everyone was staring at the board as if it were a math equation.

I went on. "And Max is the only one with Invention as a genius, and one of his competencies is Wonder."

More staring. Frowning. Calculating.

"So, as a group, you guys aren't great at coming up with new ideas or asking the right questions that might provoke a new idea." I didn't want them to think I was being harsh, so I clarified, "As a group, that's what your profile would say."

Heads were nodding, which told me I probably hadn't offended them.

Kirstin spoke next. "The way we're organized makes it so we don't have to do much Wonder or Invention. Heck, or Discernment, really."

Jasper and Quinn looked at each other and seemed embarrassed. I asked Kirstin for an explanation.

"Well," she said, a little cautiously, "by the time we get involved in a project, you guys"—she motioned at Quinn, Jasper, and me—"have already done most of the creative, big-picture thinking."

The other littles were nodding their heads.

She continued. "So, we're pretty much doing implementation work."

I asked the big question. "And how is that for you guys?" I didn't wait for an answer before clarifying my question. "Is that frustrating?"

Littles were looking around at one another to see who would go first.

Finally, Kristen spoke up. "I'd like to practice my Discernment skills more."

Now everyone but Makena was nodding.

Max spoke up. "Yeah. Don't get me wrong, because I know we all have to do grunt work, but I really want to get involved in the creative and strategic side of things someday. I think I'd be much better at that."

I nodded but didn't know exactly what to say.

Max helped me when he added, "But I have to pay my dues."

And then I responded matter-of-factly, "That's a bunch of crap."

Everyone was stunned, but most noticeably, Max.

I immediately clarified my comment. "What you said isn't crap, Max. I didn't mean that."

He started breathing again.

"What I mean is that people paying dues is bullshit. Especially if it means doing things they're not good at in order to prove that they're worthy of doing what they're great at." I paused. "Does that make sense?"

A few heads were nodding, but, surprisingly, it was Makena who resonated with what I had said more than anyone.

"Listen," she announced with a smile on her face that seemed to be a mix of passion and fear. "I love what I'm doing, right now. I'm not trying to get promoted into a job that I'm not good at."

She looked at Max. "You want to work on the more strategic and creative side of things, right?"

He nodded.

"I don't," she declared emphatically. "I realize that isn't the right thing to say, and that we're all supposed to be strategic and creative and whatever else. But I'm more of an implementer. And I would be pretty frustrated if you asked me to get involved in projects before someone else figured out the direction and plan."

I suddenly had a revelation. "This is what it was like in so many of the agencies that I knew. They hire people to do one job, and the ones who are good at it get promoted to different jobs requiring different skills. Often, they don't do well in their new jobs because they were much better suited for their old jobs, and the people who would be great at the new jobs never get promoted because they were bad at the old jobs."

Jasper was staring at me with his mouth open. "Say that again."

Everyone cracked up.

"Okay, I realize that was confusing, but do you know what I mean?"

Makena announced, "Yeah. Don't promote me to a job I don't want, and don't make me feel like a failure for doing what I'm good at now."

Kirstin added, "And don't make Max prove that he's good at something he's not in order to do what he's really good at."

Jasper was now staring at Makena and Kirstin. "Say that again."

Thankfully, he then explained, "I'm kidding. I get it. This makes complete sense."

Quinn jumped in. "The solution has to be teams."

"I think I agree," I said. "But explain what you mean."

"Well, when you put a group of people together on a project, you want to have all the geniuses covered. If you focus too much on job descriptions or experience levels, it gets screwed up."

Jasper picked up from there. "If the project needs Invention or Discernment, find someone who has that and use them. And let them spend as much of their time as possible doing those things."

I summarized. "We should be organizing more of our work— our projects, our client groups, our programs—in terms of what geniuses are needed, and doing our best to get people into the roles where they are best suited."

"What about when that isn't possible?" Quinn asked.

"It won't always be possible. Nothing ever works out that neatly. All of us have to find a way to push through and do our best when we're not in our areas of genius, or even competency.

But if that's twenty or thirty percent of the time, instead of seventy, we're all going be a lot happier. And more effective."

"So, what's next?" Jasper asked.

"What's next is the leadership team rethinking how we organize and staff and manage our work. From the top down. And maybe"—I paused—"just maybe, we'll find a way to keep Max around."

This time, Max smiled big, and I knew what I needed to focus on in the days and weeks ahead.

EVIDENCE

From that point on, I was completely convinced that this Working Genius stuff wasn't merely a convenient way to explain why I was grumpy at work. I had seen what it did for Chris and my leadership team. It had worked at church. We used it to avoid losing Max and prevent a future problem with Makena.

And if that weren't enough, Anna said it was the best thing I had ever done at work. The fact that it was an accident, and that it wasn't really part of what my firm was supposed to be doing, only diminished my enthusiasm a little.

For the next two weeks, we spent almost half our time at the office rethinking how we would work differently now that we understood and could actually describe our innate strengths and weaknesses. Every meeting we had, every conversation in the hallway, suddenly became peppered with references to Discernment and Galvanizing and Tenacity and genius and frustration. And we weren't even trying!

Within a month, morale was higher than it had been since we

had founded the agency four years earlier. But as Jasper liked to say, "Who cares about morale? What about the work?"

The fact is, we were getting more done, in less time, and having more fun than we had thought possible. Which, as I liked to say, was what morale is all about.

But, perhaps, the best way to explain the power of "The Six Types of Working Genius," as we came to call it, is to tell you about a client meeting that took place three months to the day—I went back and checked—after the model was born. Though I wish I had recorded this meeting, I'm pretty sure I was able to piece together the dialogue with more than 8 percent accuracy.

THE CLIENT MEETING

Amy and I were at St. Luke's Hospital, the largest in the area, doing our first planning session with the head of marketing and her team, as well as the CEO and the head of HR, who wanted to join us. We had also brought a larger team with us, something I had begun doing a few weeks earlier. The more genius we had in the room, the better chance we would have to avoid missing anything important.

On that particular day, we brought Max and Chris. Chris would be important because this would become one of our largest clients, and his ability to galvanize would depend on understanding what we were doing and why we were doing it. Chris had started coming to more client meetings than ever, and it made a huge difference in our coordination and follow-through.

Max was there because I needed someone else in the room who could help me invent and discern simultaneously. The St. Luke's account was going to have multiple projects, and we would need to show our clients that we could be creative and adaptable in order to earn their trust.

This kind of launch meeting would be a long one, allowing the client to lay out their needs in detail, review what they had done over the past few years, and solicit our general ideas about how we would help them. It would be strategic, much more specific than a sales call, but not a presentation of detailed messages and visuals.

The CEO, a really, really tall guy named Joseph, kicked things off by explaining that marketing and advertising at a hospital, especially one that was connected to a church, was not just about driving revenue—yes, they did have to worry about their finances—but was also about improving the hospital's brand and helping the community connect to the culture of the organization.

"We've done our research, Joseph," I told him, "but I'd like to hear from you what that culture is."

Joseph frowned, but only because he was thinking about what to say. "Well," he began, "I'm going to be honest with you. We have a list of values and a slide deck and posters around the hospital advertising our culture." He paused and glanced over at the head of HR in what I can only describe as a hint of discomfort. "But I'm not sure it's as real and true as it needs to be."

I glanced at the head of HR, a guy about my age, who now seemed a little nervous, too.

"Explain what you mean," I asked.

"Well, we tout ourselves as having a positive, optimistic, caring culture. So many hospitals do that these days. But when I walk the halls at night, and even sometimes during the day, I just don't see it or feel it."

Chris asked the question before I could. "What's the difference between the experience at night and during the day?"

Joseph smiled. "During the day more people in the hospital know who I am, and I'm pretty sure they turn it up a notch for me. At night, I can walk around here anonymously, and I think I see the reality better."

Enough people in the room nodded to confirm for me that Joseph was probably right.

Amy went next. "What exactly do you see that you don't like?"

"Well . . ." Joseph took a breath. "It's not that our people are rude or uncaring or anything like that." He thought about it. "But I can't say they seem as engaged or enthusiastic or genuinely passionate about what they're doing as I'd like. I mean, they're in the business of saving and caring for human life, which is precious, and I want them to feel that in their bones. I want patients to see that emanating from the staff."

"Do you think they're just burned out?" I asked.

He shook his head. "No. We're pretty good at spotting burnout. I mean, we have pockets of it in certain departments where we're understaffed, but it's not the norm. And when we survey people, and when I talk to people on my late-night walking tours, the ones who don't know who I am, they tell me they feel poorly utilized and frustrated."

Now the head of marketing jumped in. "We think that one of the benefits of a great marketing campaign is that it will have as much of an impact on our own people as it will on our patients and the community."

The head of HR nodded enthusiastically.

I agreed with her. "I agree with you." As I said, I'm a straight shooter that way. "But it's so important to get the reality lined up with the messaging, or it could backfire."

A few of the marketing people seemed confused, so I went on.

"Have you ever been on an airplane when they run that ridiculous video message at the beginning of the flight, right before the safety check?" I didn't wait for an answer. "They have these bright-eyed employees, or sometimes the CEO, declaring how much they care about passengers and about their company and how they are ready to do whatever they can to make your flight an amazing experience."

Now people were nodding.

"Well, how does that make you feel?"

One of the marketing people blurted out, "I don't know how to say it, exactly. But it's gross. It makes me feel like I'm being lied to."

Someone else added, "And it makes me feel bad for the employees. I always look at them, and it seems like they're doing everything they can not to roll their eyes." She shook her head. "I don't think anyone benefits from those stupid videos."

"Right," I agreed. "It makes customers and employees cynical. That's what I mean by backfire."

Now the head of marketing spoke. "I know what you're saying, but I don't think that's what's going on here. We're not that hypocritical, but we're definitely not acting the way we want the world to see us."

Finally, the head of HR spoke up. "And we're not losing people to other hospitals or other jobs. Their survey results are fine.

It's like they're staying but they've just accepted that there's only so much they can do."

That's when Max spoke up. "You guys should go through our Working Genius program."

Because Max was quite a bit younger than us, and because he had yet to speak, his words caught people's attention a little more than normal.

"Excuse me?" the head of marketing asked, genuinely curious.

A little nervous now that the attention was all on him, Max explained, "We came up with this simple tool at our office for understanding what people are naturally good at doing and what they are naturally bad at doing. It changed the way we work right away. Heck, I wouldn't be here at this meeting if we hadn't done it."

The head of HR sat up in his chair. "How long does it take?"

"Well, I'd say it changed our work culture in a few weeks or less."

"No." The HR VP smiled. "How long does it take to do the assessment?"

I jumped in now. "Oh, we don't have an assessment. We just try to figure out what we are as a group." I looked at Amy. "An assessment would be cool, though."

Now Joseph reengaged. "You said it changed the culture of your office in a few weeks?" He looked at me, just a little skeptically.

I shrugged. "It's kind of true. I mean, for some people it was immediate. But it took us a few weeks to figure out what it was and then work it through the agency."

"How long does it take to explain?" asked the HR guy.

Instinctively, I looked at the clock. We had all day, and I could do an overview in twenty minutes. I looked at Amy and she shrugged and nodded simultaneously, giving me permission to go for it.

"I could probably do it all in less than half an hour, soup to nuts."

The dozen or so clients looked at each other as if they were waiting for someone to say, "Yeah, let's do it."

And then Chris said, "It really works. Changed my career overnight."

"Then let's do it," Joseph declared, and everyone was on board.

I'm not going to lie. I had never been so excited to present something to a client in my career.

PASSION

For the next twenty-five minutes, I presented the model from beginning to end. I explained the six types of work and how they fit together. I described the differences between a person's geniuses, competencies, and frustrations. I even explained the stages of work: ideation, activation, and implementation.

Amy and Chris jumped in often to help explain a subtlety or a nuance. Even Max told his story.

I'm not lying when I say that the clients were all in about what I was presenting. They asked questions, wrestled with the concepts, and helped one another identify most of their geniuses and frustrations. At the end, Chris went to the board and wrote what we would later describe as the marketing team's "genius map."

I thought the head of HR was going to explode. Or implode. Whatever someone does when they're excited.

Even Joseph asked how he could use this with his leadership team.

An hour later, the marketing team had reorganized part of their department. As remarkable as that sounds, it was actually pretty obvious what they needed to do, but only after they realized that they had people in the wrong roles and that it was slowing everything down.

The head of HR (I should probably give him a name now—Ken—I didn't realize he'd factor into the story so much) told us he knew of a local firm who could help us put together an assessment. He wanted to help us work with the executive team, his own team, and the Chief Nursing Officer and her staff.

Finally, we went on with the marketing and advertising part of our day, which seemed so much more meaningful and intentional. And the most amazing thing of all—yes, more amazing than what had already happened—was how they had adopted the vocabulary of the genius types.

At one point, Mary, the head of marketing, said, "I'm not Galvanizing here, so don't think I'm telling you guys to go out and act on what I'm about to say. I'm just coming up with a new idea, and I need you to do the D thing—what is it? Discernment?" Wow. She had used the terms almost precisely the way they were meant to be used, and everyone knew what she meant. This was only a short time after hearing about the model!

And at the end of the day, Joseph announced to the group, "I have to tell you all that the executive team, my leadership team"—he looked at Mary and Ken, who were members—"spend almost no time in the Wonder part of work. We don't take enough time to ponder and ask questions. Instead, we dive right into implementation. It's no wonder we haven't instilled the hospital with a greater sense of the mission and the real meaning behind what we're doing."

When we closed the meeting and exchanged enthusiastic handshakes, the four of us went to the parking lot to debrief.

As the doors to Amy's minivan closed, Chris went first.

"What just happened?" He seemed genuinely confused.

"Is that how these meetings usually go?" Max asked, in humor.

Amy just started laughing.

"Has anyone here had that much fun at work before?" It was a rhetorical question. "I don't even know how to describe that."

Amy just kept laughing.

STAFF MEETING

The next morning, I couldn't wait to tell Quinn, Jasper, and Lynne about what had happened the day before. Unfortunately, Chris arrived earlier than I did and beat me to the punch.

Of course, Amy and I had plenty to add once the meeting started, and even though they hadn't been with us at the hospital, the rest of the team seemed more excited than I would have thought.

And Jasper had a story of his own.

"My band did the Working Genius last night, and we decided to break up."

Jasper was the bass player of a classic rock band based in Reno, called Instant Replay, that played original songs and covers for parties and corporate gigs. Oddly enough, he didn't seem too upset about what happened to his band.

"Yeah, we've been pretty miserable for the past year or so, and we didn't know why. As it turns out, four of us have the Genius of Invention. I'm the only one who doesn't."

"Why is that a problem?" Lynne asked.

"Because they all want to write songs and be the leader of the band. They still think they're going to make it, and I'm fine standing in the background, playing the bass, and watching people have a great time."

"So, you're retiring?" Amy asked.

"Nah. I'll probably just find a band that needs a bass player and has a little more balance. Less drama."

"Are the guys upset?" I wondered.

"You know . . ." Jasper thought about it. "They were pretty clear about it all. I mean, when they agreed that they were all inventors, they admitted that it wouldn't work." He frowned. "To be honest, I think they were kind of relieved."

Chris brought the conversation to a close. "Okay, everyone. Let's get started. We have a bit of a problem, a good problem, but a problem nonetheless."

He had our attention.

"Two of our clients are asking for more work from us. A lot more work. And I don't think we'll be able to get it all done with our current staff."

I tried to make light of the situation. "Hey, now that Jasper's out of the band, he'll have more time."

Everyone but Chris thought it was funny.

"Bull, here's the thing. You and Amy have been out there selling like crazy lately. And that's great." He paused. "I mean, that was fantastic yesterday."

He took a longer pause than normal, and I could tell he was afraid to say what he was thinking.

"Come on, Chris. Spit it out. It's okay."

"Well, I'm not sure you really appreciate what it takes to execute on all of your ideas."

I wasn't at all upset by what he said, so I did my best to sound open. "What do you mean by appreciation?"

"Well . . ." He paused again. "You often underestimate what goes into the implementation part of work."

I was so relieved! "Okay, I get that. And I agree. I definitely do that. I was afraid you were saying that I don't appreciate the people who do that work."

Jasper jumped in. "No, I know you appreciate them. But I agree that you often dismiss our concerns about workload and what it will take to get things done."

Quinn came to my defense. "I think it's because his geniuses are Invention and Discernment."

"And his frustrations are Enablement and Tenacity," Jasper added.

"Which is not an excuse," Quinn reminded me, "but it makes sense."

I was nodding my head, feeling a little embarrassed. "I know, I know. I tend to think that the work will just get done. That's on me. Besides being more aware of it, what can I do to help?"

"You can let us hire more people with E and T," he said, knowing that we'd all know what he meant. He went on. "I know you like to keep things lean around here, and that we've always been able to find a way, but things are starting to take off, and we have to get ahead of the problem."

I have to admit, it made sense to me. But I think my modest

upbringing made me afraid of spending too much and regretting it later. Until the right person spoke.

"I agree with him." It was Lynne. "My gut tells me that we're about to stumble if we don't bring on a handful of people who can crank."

Quinn raised her hand and spoke. "I agree completely."

Two of the people on my team with Discernment were in agreement, and though my fears gave me pause, my instincts told me Chris was right. If I believed in the Working Genius, and I did, how could I deny the veracity of what I was hearing?

"Do it."

Chris seemed surprised.

I repeated myself. "Let's hire five new people. And let's make sure that most of them have Tenacity or Enablement as geniuses. We could probably use a galvanizer, too."

"Wow," Chris said. "It usually takes a lot longer than that to convince you of something like this."

I agreed. "Yeah, and that's my bad. This makes sense, and there's no reason to wait."

Amy had a question. "How do we go about finding people based on their geniuses? Even if we had an assessment already, is that even legal?"

"Technically, no," Chris explained. "You're not supposed to give people an assessment before you decide to hire them. It might be biased or discriminatory, or something like that."

"But if it helps you and that person figure out if they're going to be successful, isn't that a good thing?" Jasper asked.

Chris just shrugged.

"That's okay. We don't need an assessment for this," Quinn declared. "Let's just explain to them exactly what they'll be doing, and let's not oversell it and make it sound easy."

Amy frowned at her, confused.

She went on. "We'll be so transparent with people about the work, the detail, the support, the follow-through, and the"—Quinn paused—"the Tenacity that they'll run screaming if they don't love it."

"But don't you think we might scare people off?" Amy asked.

"Do you think Makena or Chris or Jasper would be scared off if we did that?"

Amy looked at Chris and Jasper.

They were shaking their heads and smiling.

"I'd be so excited to take that job," Jasper said. "The right people will opt in, and the others won't. It's ridiculously simple, and I think it will work. Why would someone want to take a job that sounds miserable? And if they try to fake it, we'll know. 'Tell me, Mr. or Mrs. Job Candidate, why you like to push through obstacles, focus on details, grind out the end of a project even when everyone else is thinking about the next project. Because if you don't love doing that, you're going to hate this job, and we're going to be frustrated with you. But if you like doing that stuff, you'll be happy as a pig in slop.'"

We laughed.

I added, "And go ahead and explain the Six Types of Working Genius to them and let them know we're looking for people in the last two. That can't be illegal. It's just honest."

And that's what we did. Within three months, we had hired

six new people—yes, more than we thought we needed—and within weeks, we knew we had found the right ones. We had never done a better job focusing on the skills we needed and identifying them in the people we interviewed. And we'd never hire again without using the Six Types of Working Genius.

LEAPFROG

Within a year, two amazing things happened, which we could never have foreseen.

First, the firm doubled in size, and quadrupled in revenue. And we were turning down work.

Second, at least a third of our work integrated the Working Genius model.

But it was another year later when everything really changed. And it began with what we now refer to as "the call."

It was early in the morning and the only people in the office were Lynne, Bella, and me. Bella didn't usually route calls to me, but Lynne was in the restroom.

"This is Bull. How can I help you?"

"Hi, Bull, my name is Kathryn and I wanted to see if you would work with our company."

"All right, Kathryn. Tell me about your company."

"Well, we're a tech company in the Bay Area. I've heard great things about your firm, and I think we could use your help."

"That's nice to hear. So, Kathryn, are you the head of marketing?"

"No, I'm the CEO."

"Wow," I said. "Usually it's the head of marketing that calls us first."

"Really?" Kathryn replied, and even over the phone I could tell she was confused. "That surprises me."

"Well," I explained, "most CEOs let their marketing VPs choose the vendors they use for marketing and advertising."

"Oh," she said, "I'm not calling you for marketing help. I thought you were productivity consultants."

Before I could completely digest what she said, I tried to respond. "Oh no, we're a boutique agency that focuses on—"

And that's when it hit me.

"Wait a second, Kathryn. What exactly are you looking for?"

"Well, I heard from a CEO friend who runs a company in Reno about the six kinds of genius at work, or something like that. He said it was amazing, and that it's exactly what I need."

I was stunned. "So you don't need any help with marketing?"

"No," she said confidently. "We're all good there. But our productivity and morale are down, and we don't know what to do. Can you help us?"

And that's the day Jeremiah Marketing became Jeremiah Consulting, with two divisions: Marketing and Advertising, which was our initial offering, and Workplace Transformation, which focused on productivity, teamwork, and staffing.

When I announced all this to Anna that night, she said something that turned out to be more accurate than I could have known. "You know, Bull, I'm guessing that a lot more companies out there need help with their people than they do with their marketing."

Though part of me wanted to, I couldn't disagree with my wife. And I couldn't wait to get started.

EPILOGUE

Ten years after the advent of Jeremiah Consulting, our Workplace Transformation division was no less than ten times the size of our Marketing and Advertising arm. With the increasing shortage of labor in the market, we found that the demand for evaluating, retaining, and motivating good employees became more competitively critical than at any time in the modern history of work.

As a result, I spent the majority of my time drilling into that part of the business, not only to grow it and help our clients, but to apply those principles to our own people. And I can honestly say that I loved my job more than ever in my career, and I almost never felt cranky at work.

Best of all, the Working Genius pervaded every part of my life. Anna and I avoided unnecessary guilt around having no Tenacity between us, and we learned how to use others to help us with projects and responsibilities that we find difficult. We also worked hard to understand the geniuses and frustrations of our children, adjusting our parenting styles and expectations accordingly. Tension in the house decreased dramatically. How I wish I had done this a decade earlier! And as we prepared for some sort of semi-retirement—I love my work too much to spend twelve hours a day golfing and fishing—Anna and I decided to organize our activities to best suit our geniuses.

At the end of the day, I've come to believe more than ever that work is meant to be dignifying and fulfilling for everyone, and that God created each of us to contribute in unique ways. And more than anything else, Working Genius has allowed me to put some handles on how I can best contribute to my company, my team, and my family.

Beyond the day-to-day activities of work and life, I, Jeremiah Octavian Brooks, now have a deep sense that I have done and am continuing to do what God created me to do. And I go about all of this with gratitude, because I know that every part of it, every single part, is a gift.

EXPLORING THE MODEL

CONTEXT

BACKSTORY

When I was a young child, I remember my dad frequently coming home at night frustrated by something he called work. And though I didn't really understand what work was, this really bothered me and I felt bad for him.

It wasn't until I started working myself that I learned that jobs were often a source of frustration for people, and that the causes of this included bad managers, poor company leadership, broken relationships with colleagues, and people having to do jobs that didn't match their natural talents and gifts.

Well, I have been blessed to have spent much of my career trying to help people find dignity and fulfillment in their work through better management, leadership, and teamwork. But I can say that I never expected to do anything novel in the area of helping them understand and align gifts with their work. Until June 2020.

I had been struggling off and on for years with my own job

dissatisfaction, which puzzled me because I had started my company with good friends, I loved the field I worked in, and I was genuinely fond of my colleagues. Still, I found myself unexplainably exhausted and exasperated on a semi-regular basis.

On that June morning, after a series of meetings that caused my job satisfaction to rise and fall and rise again in the course of an hour, my colleague Amy asked me the big question: "Why are you like this?" For some reason, I decided that would be a good time to take a stab at diagnosing my struggle. And that led to a four-hour conversation during which I inadvertently came up with the Six Types of Working Genius.

As soon as the rough model made its way onto the whiteboard in my office, the light bulbs started flashing in my brain. Big parts of my life started to make more sense.

For instance, I finally understood why, as a child, I gladly did some of the chores assigned to me by my parents, and resisted others. I now knew why, in college, the clock seemed to move quickly during some of my courses, and why it ground to a halt and even seemed to move backward in many others. And I could even explain why I failed in my first job in the real world, and why I flourished in others. But best of all, I knew the reasons that I was often frustrated in my current situation, at work and in life. It was nothing short of a massive personal breakthrough.

Since that day, my team and I have worked to transform those first insights into an individual assessment, which more than a quarter of a million people have already used to identify their geniuses and improve their careers and their teams. We've also created a podcast dedicated to Working Genius, a certification program for trainers who want to teach and use Working Genius in their own practices and companies, and a team tool to help groups use Working Genius to transform how they work together.

And, finally, I have written this book to better explain it all.

DEFINING WORK

Before I get into the model itself, I need to clarify that *work* is a broad term that applies to almost every part of our lives, even beyond what we formally refer to as jobs. Whether we're starting a company, launching a new product, providing support for customers, organizing a nonprofit, running a food pantry at church, or planning a family vacation, we're working. We're getting things done.

Given that broad definition, it wouldn't be a stretch to say that the majority of our waking hours involve some kind of work, sometimes alone, more often with others.

I believe that all work should be dignifying and satisfying, both in terms of the experience itself, and the fruit it produces. And while every type of work involves doing things that are less than exhilarating and, at times, somewhat tedious or frustrating, anything we can do to help ourselves and others make the most of work is worthwhile.

The first and most important step in doing this is understanding that each of us enjoys different kinds of work, and then figuring out which kind suits us best. If we go through life without an understanding of our natural gifts, the best we can hope for is to be lucky enough to find ourselves doing what we love. The Working Genius, first and foremost, is a means for allowing anyone to identify those gifts. It all starts there.

Now let's take a thorough look at the model.

MODEL AND ASSESSMENT

THE SIX TYPES DEFINED

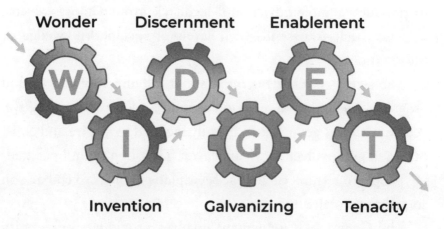

The Genius of *Wonder* involves the ability to ponder and speculate and question the state of things, asking the questions that provoke answers and action. People with this genius are naturally inclined to do these things. They find it easy to lose themselves in observing the world around them and wondering whether things shouldn't be different or whether there is untapped potential that should be tapped.

The Genius of *Invention* is all about coming up with new ideas and solutions. People with this genius are drawn toward origination, creativity, and ingenuity in the truest sense of those words, even with little direction and context. Though every type is a genius, these are the people who are most often referred to as "geniuses" because many of their ideas seem to come out of thin air.

The Genius of *Discernment* is related to instinct, intuition, and uncanny judgment. People with this genius have a natural ability to assess an idea or situation, even without a lot of data or expertise. Using pattern recognition and gut feel, they are able to provide valuable advice and feedback around most subjects in a way that transcends their levels of specific knowledge or information.

The Genius of *Galvanizing* is about rallying, motivating, and provoking people to take action around an idea or an initiative. People with this genius are naturally inclined to inspire and enlist others to get involved in an endeavor. They don't mind persuading people to rethink or change their plans in order to embark on something worthwhile.

The Genius of *Enablement* involves providing people with support and assistance in the way that it is needed. People with this genius are adept at responding to the needs of others without conditions or restrictions. They are naturally inclined to help others accomplish their goals and often can anticipate what people might need before they even ask. Individuals with the Genius of Enablement are frequently unaware that this is a genius at all.

The Genius of *Tenacity* is about the satisfaction of pushing things across the finish line to completion. People with this genius are not only capable of, but naturally inclined to, finish projects and ensure that they are completed according to specification. They gain energy by pushing through obstacles and seeing the impact of their work, and they find joy in crossing tasks off their list and getting closure.

GENIUS VS. COMPETENCY VS. FRUSTRATION

Even though each type is called a genius, no one person can claim all six as their individual geniuses. We all have areas where we thrive, areas where we struggle, and areas that fall somewhere in between. Let's take a look at each of those three categories, because success requires us to understand the areas where we shine as well as those where we don't.

Category 1: Working Genius
Each of us has two areas that are considered our true geniuses. These are the activities that give us joy, energy, and passion. As a result, we are usually quite good in these areas. It's best for us and the organizations we serve if we can do much, if not most, of our work in these areas.

Category 2: Working Competency
Two of the six areas of genius would be considered our working competencies. These are the activities that we find neither completely miserable nor completely joyful, and which we can

do fairly well, perhaps even very well. Most of us can manage to operate in our working competencies fairly well for a while, but we will eventually grow weary if we are not allowed to exercise our true geniuses.

Category 3: Working Frustration

Finally, each of us has two types of work that drain us of our joy and energy, and we call these our working frustrations. We usually struggle in these activities. Of course, no one can completely avoid working in our areas of frustration from time to time, but if we find ourselves spending meaningful time engaged in these activities, we are bound to experience misery at work, and ultimately, struggle or even fail.

It's worth asking the question here, why do people have two geniuses, rather than one, or three? Because that's how the thousands of people who tested the model encountered it, time and time again. For every person who initially thought that they *might* have more than two geniuses, there were ninety-nine who settled on two. And in so many cases, when we asked the people who thought they might have three geniuses (one person even claimed to have all six!) about where they received *energy and joy,* they settled on two.

A good way to understand the difference between our Working Geniuses, competencies, and frustrations is to think about coffee, and how it retains heat and energy.

Working Genius is like a thermos that we fill with hot coffee and then tightly put a lid over it. The heat and energy in that thermos will last for a long, long time. Similarly, when we work within our geniuses, we can stay energized and motivated almost indefinitely.

Working Competency is more like pouring coffee into a regular cup and putting a plastic lid on it, or perhaps no lid at all. The coffee will stay hot for a while, but eventually, it will grow cooler and finally cold. When we work within our areas of working competency, we can sustain a level of energy for a while, but eventually we will see it dissipate, and we will begin to lose steam.

Working Frustration would be like pouring coffee into a cup, but one that has a small hole in its bottom. The heat of that coffee, even the coffee itself, will last for a very short period of time. When we work in our areas of frustration, it's difficult to sustain a level of passion or energy for any length of time.

RESPONSIVE VS. DISRUPTIVE GENIUSES

Another important way to look at the Six Types of Working Genius is in terms of whether a given genius is primarily responsive or disruptive. This is important because *responsive* geniuses tend to, well, respond to an external stimulus in order to be put into action. These might also be referred to as restrained compared to their disruptive counterparts. *Disruptive* geniuses, on the other hand, generally initiate or provoke change when they see a need for it, even if others aren't necessarily calling for it. They are more proactive in the way they interact with a project or initiative.

Some people will have two responsive geniuses, meaning they

might be a little more reluctant to initiate activity. Some will have two disruptive geniuses, making them more likely to provoke action. Of course, some will have one of each type.

Understand that this mix of responsive and disruptive can be helpful in confirming our areas of genius when we are unsure. It's also important in helping us understand why people interact with their environment in a certain way, which helps us avoid making inaccurate or judgmental assessments about their attitude or aptitude.

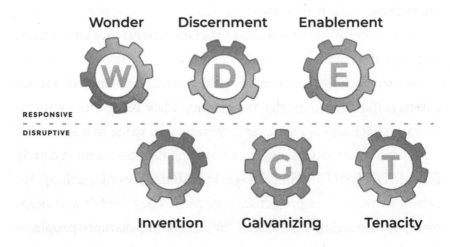

The three *responsive* geniuses include Wonder, Discernment, and Enablement.

People with the Wonder genius respond to their environment, observing the organization, industry, or world around them in order to generate questions. They don't necessarily set out to change the world around them. They simply behold it, take it in, and let their observations unfold.

Those with Discernment respond to the ideas or proposals of

inventors, providing feedback, advice, or counsel. They are a big part of the innovation process but aren't necessarily the ones to provoke it. Beyond innovation, they often respond to, and even curate, whatever the world puts in front of them.

Those with Enablement respond to the stated requests of others, most often someone Galvanizing for support. They are ready to provide what is needed, and are even so good at surmising what is desired that they begin to provide it before it has been completely specified or requested. But they don't generally initiate support until it is needed.

The three *disruptive* geniuses include Invention, Galvanizing, and Tenacity.

People with Invention see a problem and come up with a novel solution that will defy the status quo. They relish the opportunity to create useful havoc, and thereby add value to a situation.

Those with Galvanizing as a Working Genius are most clearly disruptive. They initiate change by rallying people, calling for others to enlist in a project or program. They recruit and organize and inspire others, which, by definition, disrupts people to shift their priorities around what needs to be done.

Those with Tenacity disrupt by identifying obstacles or roadblocks and pushing through them. They are determined to complete a project regardless of what stands in the way. They bring about whatever change is necessary to achieve success, regardless of what needs to be disrupted in the process.

It is common for people to value disruptive genius over the responsive kind. Of course, this is incorrect and dangerous. The responsive and disruptive geniuses alternate in the course of work, creating a kind of balance and synergy that is necessary. Without the question or observation of Wonder, for instance, there is no need for Invention. And without Discernment of an inventor's idea, that original concept will be far less likely to succeed. And without Enablement, the most persuasive galvanizer will not get a program off the ground. There is no doubt that responsive and disruptive geniuses are equally valuable in the process of effective work.

Now that we've done a relatively thorough overview of the model and a few of its nuances, let's take a look at an example of one person's Working Genius Assessment report.

ASSESSMENT AND REPORT

By far the most effective way to discover a person's geniuses, competencies, and frustrations is to complete the Working Genius Assessment and review the report that is generated instantly from it.

The assessment itself is a forty-two-question survey that takes about ten minutes to complete. Immediately upon completing the assessment, users receive a report providing results from the assessment and guidance about how to interpret and qualitatively confirm the accuracy. Even though this is a quantitative process, it is always important for users to understand the model in the rare case that their results don't accurately reflect their Working Geniuses. This could happen because they completed the assessment incorrectly or with an incorrect understanding of the question. Again, this is rare, but it's worth taking an additional few minutes to review the descriptions of each genius.

The best way to understand the report is to review one; let's use mine as an example.

WHAT YOUR QUANTITATIVE RESULTS INDICATE

☝ WORKING GENIUS:

Your *likely* areas of Working Genius are **Invention** and **Discernment**.

 You are naturally gifted at and derive energy and joy from creating original and novel ideas and solutions.

 You are naturally gifted at and derive energy and joy from using your intuition and instincts to evaluate and assess ideas or plans.

☝ WORKING COMPETENCY:

Your *likely* areas of Working Competency are **Wonder** and **Galvanizing**.

 You are capable of and don't mind pondering the possibility of greater potential and opportunity in a given situation.

 You are capable of and don't mind rallying people and inspiring them to take action around a project, task or idea.

⚲ WORKING FRUSTRATION:

Your *likely* areas of Working Frustration are **Tenacity** and **Enablement**.

 You *aren't* naturally gifted at and/or derive energy and joy from pushing projects and tasks through to completion to ensure that the desired results are achieved.

 You *aren't* naturally gifted at and/or derive energy and joy from providing others with encouragement and assistance for projects and ideas.

As you can see, my two Working Geniuses (the activities from which I derive joy and energy and that most would consider my greatest strengths) are called Invention and Discernment. Invention indicates that I love coming up with new ideas. Generating new proposals, products, and ideas out of nothing is very comfortable for me. In fact, I prefer to do it from scratch. Discernment indicates that I also love evaluating ideas. I rely on my intuitive judgment to make evaluations and decisions, even when I have limited data or domain expertise. I trust my gut, and others do, too.

It would be my dream job for people to come to me all day long with an important problem that needed to be solved, and to let me come up with a novel solution out of thin air. That's when I'm at my best. I would also love for people to come to me with their own ideas, and ask me to evaluate them using my gut feel and instincts. I am blessed to be able to do a lot of this kind of work in my current role. As you can imagine, coming up with this model, and refining it, was a party!

My two working competencies (the activities that I don't mind doing and in which I am somewhat competent) are Galvanizing and Wonder. Galvanizing means I can rally people around a new initiative or idea fairly well, and Wonder means I don't mind pondering and contemplating the state of things in an organization or the world. Nonetheless, because these are not my Working Geniuses, too much of these activities eventually leaves me exhausted.

I know this because, for years, I was the primary, if not the only, galvanizer in my organization. Everyone thought I performed that role because I enjoyed Galvanizing, but I was simply filling a gap. And because it was preventing me from doing what I loved most (Invention and Discernment), it eventually began to crush me. As for Wonder, I don't mind doing it for a while, but I *quickly* get impatient contemplating things and want to move toward inventing a solution, even when more wondering might be necessary.

Finally, my two working frustrations (the areas that drain me of energy and joy) are Enablement and Tenacity. Enablement means I don't enjoy and am not very good at assisting others with projects *on their terms*, and Tenacity means I don't like, and am not good at, pushing a project or initiative through to the end after the idea stage has ended. Though I certainly have to do Enablement and Tenacity activities sometimes, I derive little satisfaction from them and will burn out quickly if I stay in those activities for long. Moreover, I will be tempted to look for ways to use my Invention and Discernment to provide assistance and finish work, even when it is not advisable or necessary.

I have to admit that it's hard to acknowledge that I am frustrated by Enablement. It makes me feel like I'm not a nice guy. The thing is, I really like to help people, but I have a hard time not using my Invention and Discernment in the helping. When someone (and I say this with apologies to my wife, Laura) asks me to do something precisely the way he or she wants it done, I wither. That's not an excuse but merely an explanation of how I'm wired. Others do this quite well and easily, and I have sincere admiration for them. As for Tenacity, I am notorious for wanting to move on to the next thing before the last one has been completed. In fact, as I'm writing this part of this book, I've just begun writing the beginning of my next one. My editor, Tracy, is not particularly happy about that. Sorry, Tracy.

Today, I try to spend as much of my time as possible inventing and discerning. I gladly step in when either Galvanizing or

Wonder is required, though I am careful to ensure that others with those geniuses are encouraged to do that kind of work more than me. And I do my best to avoid having to use Enablement or Tenacity, but when it is inevitable, I try to grind it out knowing that I'll be back to inventing and discerning soon enough.

As for whether my geniuses are disruptive or responsive, we can see that I have one in each category. I am disruptive because one of my geniuses is Invention, which means I come up with ideas that will bring about change. But I am also responsive because one of my geniuses is Discernment, which means I react to the ideas and proposals of others. So, I have something of a balance in these areas. Some people will find that both of their geniuses fall within the category of either disruption or responsiveness, and in these cases, the disruptive vs. responsive impact will be more pronounced.

That is a pretty quick but thorough overview of how Working Genius describes one person—in this case, me. However, how I interact with others on my team is a much bigger, and just as important, issue. In the next section, we're going to explore all of that.

TEAM PRODUCTIVITY AND MAP

THREE PHASES OF WORK

What sets the Six Types of Working Genius apart from other tools is its application to the specific activities involved in any kind of group work. As such, it is extremely actionable for people who lead teams, projects, and organizations.

I think it's worth understanding that, as I was coming up with the Working Genius model, and before I fully understood the six types, I initially identified three phases of work. It was from those phases that the six types emerged.

Let's take a quick look at each of those phases before we explore the six types within the context of teams.

The first stage of work, *Ideation*, is comprised of both Wonder and Invention. This is the part of work associated with identifying needs and proposing solutions. Innovation is most often connected with this stage. Even before Invention can take place, someone must ask the big question or identify a need. This is the first critical step in any kind of work, and provides the context for Invention.

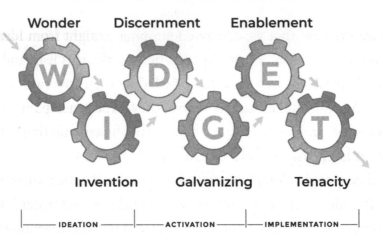

The second stage of work, *Activation*, is comprised of Discernment and Galvanizing. This part of work is about evaluating the merits of the ideas or solutions proposed during Ideation, and then rallying people around the ideas or solutions that are worthy of action. Most organizations aren't even aware that this stage exists (which I'll address below), which leaves them to jump from the first stage, Ideation, to the third and final one . . .

The third and final stage of work, *Implementation*, is comprised of Enablement and Tenacity, and is all about getting things done. Whether it is answering the call to action or pushing that action through to the final stages of completion, these genius types are the ones who ensure that great ideas, the ones that have been discerned and galvanized, actually come to fruition.

The Missing Piece

Now, as I alluded to earlier, the most important part of understanding these three phases is recognizing that the Activation phase exists so that we can avoid jumping straight from Ideation to Implementation. When organizations make this leap and skip over Activation, they are often puzzled by their low rates of success. And, to make matters worse, they experience painful, unnecessary, and unproductive blame and finger-pointing. Here's how it happens.

The people doing ideation get frustrated when their ideas don't come to fruition, and they blame the implementers, wondering why they can't execute on their fantastic inventions. At the same time, the implementers are frustrated with the lack of success, and they wonder why the ideators don't give them better ideas to implement in the first place. This is all too common in many organizations.

Without proper activation, even good ideas won't get properly vetted, modified, and improved (Discernment), and people won't be properly educated and inspired (Galvanizing). Simply by understanding the nature and importance of activation, many teams are able to realize immediate and significant improvement in the success of their initiatives.

THE SIX REQUIRED ACTIVITIES FOR ANY KIND OF TEAM-BASED WORK

Ultimately, every collective endeavor involves—and requires—each of the six geniuses. If even one of them is lacking, failure and frustration become much more likely. As such, each type of genius gives something one of the other geniuses needs. In turn, it receives something from another genius. That's why we decided to present the model as a series of gears with interdependent teeth. (That was actually my wife's idea. Thank you, Laura!)

Let's take a look at how each of the geniuses fits within the general flow of any type of work endeavor.

Wonder

The first stage of work calls for someone to ask a big question, ponder the possibility of greater potential, raise a red flag, or simply speculate about the state of things. "Is there a better way?" "Is this the best company we can be?" "Does anyone else feel like something is wrong with the way we deal with customers?" "Do we need a vacation?"

Invention

The next stage involves answering that question by creating a solution, coming up with a plan, proposing a new idea, or devising a novel approach. "I have an idea!" "How does this plan sound?" "What if we helped customers like this?" "Let's go somewhere within driving distance, like the Napa Valley!"

Discernment

The third stage is all about responding to and evaluating the idea that comes from Invention. It involves assessing the proposal, providing feedback about the solution, or tweaking the approach. "My gut tells me that would be a great idea." "I have a strong feeling that something's not quite right about those values." "I think we need to tweak your product idea a little more before it's ready." "Monterey Bay has better weather this time of year if we want to spend time outside."

Galvanizing

Once that plan or solution has been vetted and is judged to be worthwhile, the next step calls for someone to rally people around it, enlist them to help implement it, or inspire them to embrace it. "Hey, everyone, listen to her idea!" "Let's all rally around these values." "Who's ready to help us make the customer service program work?" "Okay, everyone, clear your schedules because we're going to Monterey."

Enablement

Next, someone has to answer that call to action, to make themselves available, to agree to do what is needed to get the solution off the ground and moving forward. "I'm on board to help with that idea." "Count me in with those values." "I'd love to help with customers; let me know when you need me." "I'll drive to Monterey, and I can take six people in my car."

Tenacity

Finally, someone has to complete the project, finish the program, push through obstacles to ensure that the work is done to specification. "Let's keep pushing because this new idea isn't a reality yet." "Okay, let's wrap this up and lock in on the values so we can send them to the board for approval by tonight's deadline." "Move over, I'll finish the customer database for you." "I know a guy who works at that hotel. I'll call him right now about booking a block of rooms and securing a discount."

Here is an oversimplified review of how all this works: the W identifies the need for change, the I creates the solution, the D evaluates and refines the solution and recommends it for action, the G rallies people for action, the E provides support and human capital, and the T makes sure the work gets accomplished and achieves the desired results.

Of course, work never fits neatly into a completely logical, linear, and orderly process. It's much messier than that. What's most important to remember is that, in one way or another, every team project, every group program, every collective endeavor involves these six activities, and that they generally come about in this order.

GENIUS GAPS

When a group of people embarks on any type of work, it is essential that each of the six types of genius be adequately available. Let's take a look at what can happen when any one of the geniuses is missing.

Lack of Wonder can lead to a team failing to take time to step back and ponder what is going on around them. Cultural issues, market opportunities, and looming problems might get overlooked in the pursuit of more pressing issues.

Lack of Invention on a team presents obvious problems. In many cases, teams start to feel a bit crazy because they know their old ways of doing things aren't working, but they find themselves stuck trying the same approaches again and again to no avail. Einstein would call this one of the definitions of insanity.

Lack of Discernment is a big problem on teams, but it's often hard to notice. That's because Discernment isn't easy to observe or identify, or, for that matter, to prove. But that doesn't make it any less real. When a team lacks this genius, it finds itself over-relying on data and models to make decisions that are best made using simple judgment. They often find themselves puzzled as they look back on bad decisions and wonder how they could have whiffed so badly.

Lack of Galvanizing on a team is relatively easy to identify as it is one of the more observable geniuses. When no one is rallying the troops or provoking action, even great ideas don't come to fruition, and the team's potential remains untapped. In these situations, you'll hear people say, "We have so many great ideas, but no one around here seems excited by them."

Lack of Enablement on a team is an obvious problem, but it can get overlooked because people too often fail to see Enablement as a genius at all. But when a team lacks it, there is a sense of frustration that no one is pitching in to help, and that no one is adequately responding to the pleas of the galvanizer. Enablement can be seen as the glue on a team, brought about by people who get joy and energy from answering the call to help. If it is lacking on a team, success is unlikely. Even the most senior executive team needs members who know how to respond to a call to action, and to provide support to help the team move forward, at every level.

Lack of Tenacity on a team is another obvious problem because programs and projects and things in general don't get finished without it. Many start-ups are filled with people with the Geniuses of Wonder, Invention, Discernment, and Galvanizing, but without someone with the Genius of Tenacity, no one jumps over hurdles and pushes through obstacles during the critical later stages of work. Every successful team, at every level, needs people who simply enjoy seeing things completed.

Filling the Gaps

There are a few ways a team can go about filling any gaps it may have relative to the six types. First, it can *hire* people who possess the genius that is missing. Of course, that is not always possible or immediately practical. Second, a team can *borrow* someone from within the organization. For instance, it can invite an outsider who has the missing genius to attend important meetings and contribute when necessary. Third, the team can *find people within the team who have the missing genius in their areas of competency*, and rely on them to fill the gap. But this should be a temporary solution as it can eventually result in burnout and resentment.

ELEVATION

Yet another interesting way to look at the geniuses is in terms of the different levels of elevation in which they occur. In the theoretical process of work, things begin "in the clouds" and generally "descend" in a sequential order until the work is finished "on the ground."

Let's take a look at how elevation works before explaining the practical benefit of it.

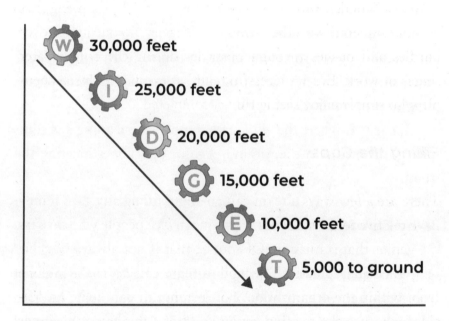

Wonder takes place at the highest elevation, with our head in the proverbial clouds. Pondering and questioning and speculating happens long before, and high above, the place and time where the rubber meets the road, if you will.

Invention comes a little lower in elevation, but still quite high. Once a question is posed or a need is addressed, Invention kicks in, but still long before and well above implementation.

Discernment takes the idea just a bit lower than Invention, assessing the practicality and usefulness of the idea or proposal. After this vetting takes place, the idea or endeavor is getting closer to the "ground" (aka implementation).

Galvanizing comes next, marshaling the human capital needed for implementation and buy-in. People are inspired, recruited, enlisted, and organized for support. Things are getting pretty close to the ground now.

Enabling is where implementation begins, with people pitching in and getting an initiative or endeavor rolling. It is the beginning of the final stage of work.

Tenacity is where the work gets completed, meaning it is completely finished. On the ground. Again, the rubber meeting the road.

Why Elevation Matters

There are times at work, during meetings, or even in the midst of projects when we skip from one elevation to another. Thinking of this as a sort of "turbulence" is helpful as we apply this model to our teams. We've all been in a brainstorming session before, with our heads in the clouds thinking up ideas, basically living in the 25,000–30,000 foot range of elevation. And suddenly a well-meaning individual on the team begins talking about tactics and how we are going to execute the plan. This is disorienting. Our plane just dropped 20,000 feet in a matter of minutes. As a result, we have to use a significant amount of brainpower and emotional energy to fight that sudden drop in elevation, then pull the plane back up to 25,000 feet so we can continue brainstorming.

Similarly, a team might be 90 percent of the way through a project and firmly in the Enablement and Tenacity phase of work (ten thousand feet to ground level) when a wonderer or inventor grabs the proverbial flight controls and says something like, "Are we sure this is the right plan?" or "I have a new idea!" Suddenly the plane rises twenty thousand feet in elevation minutes before we thought we were landing it. Get the barf bags ready because everyone is about to get dizzy and sick.

WORK CONVERSATIONS

Whenever we sit down with others to get work done, we need to understand and agree on the context of that work and the nature of the conversations we are having if we want to be productive and avoid unnecessary confusion. Generally speaking, there are four different kinds of work conversations, and they correspond to different clusters of Working Geniuses.

Brainstorming

The least frequent but often first part of work conversations involves asking questions, pondering opportunities, suggesting ideas, and evaluating whether or not those ideas might work.

This is called brainstorming, and it involves the first three Working Geniuses, Wonder, Invention, and Discernment. When everyone at the table understands this, they can stay within those geniuses and avoid drifting to others that are not yet relevant. When people go to brainstorming sessions and try to engage in Galvanizing, Enablement, or Tenacity, they often become frustrated—and frustrate others—by trying to drive discussions toward action before that is appropriate. People whose geniuses lie in the G, E, and T can often find themselves impatient during these discussions, wondering why the people with W, I, and D don't just make a decision and move on. In these situations, they need to intentionally avoid pulling the conversation into their areas of comfort, and if that doesn't work, avoid taking part in these conversations entirely (though I recommend this only as a last resort).

Decision-making

Another type of work conversation has to do with coming to a decision related to a proposed idea or proposal. These discussions are centered around Discernment, but they also involve some levels of Invention ("let's tweak the idea a little") and Galvanizing ("let's think about how we would get people on board"). During these sessions, it's a good idea to avoid Wonder, as the time for that kind of conversation has ended. It's also important to avoid the temptation to begin implementation, which involves Enablement and Tenacity, as those geniuses may tempt people to settle for a suboptimal decision simply to gain closure.

Launch

The next type of work conversation is about getting people excited about a decision and enlisted in its initial actions. This is centered around Galvanizing and Enablement but involves Discernment, too, as questions arise from people who are trying to understand what they are signing up to do. Wonder and Invention should certainly be avoided in these discussions as much as possible, as the time for those geniuses has passed. Tenacity is not yet fully engaged but needs to be present because organizing a new project without the perspective of what will be required to finish it is a recipe for unnecessary confusion down the road.

Status Review and Problem-Solving

The final type of conversation that happens at work is the one that happens most frequently, usually during staff meetings. It involves regular discussions about the progress of an initiative, as well as the identification and resolution of any obstacles or problems that stand in the way of completion. This centers around Galvanizing (and re-Galvanizing) and Enablement, and finally, Tenacity. When team members try to exercise Wonder or Invention during this part of work, they usually create chaos and frustration. Even Discernment should be limited to the process of overcoming tactical obstacles rather than reevaluating the original idea or proposal.

The key to all of this is constantly checking in with team members about the purpose of a given discussion (or meeting) and making sure that the required geniuses are present or represented during each of those sessions. For instance, if everyone is clear and aligned with what they are meant to be doing, people will draw upon their appropriate geniuses and avoid jumping forward or back to geniuses that are not relevant or helpful.

USING THE TEAM MAP

One of the most powerful, and simple, ways for applying Working Genius to groups of people is using something that we call the Team Map. Essentially, this is a visual portrayal of the collective geniuses and frustrations of team members, which allows us to better understand one another, and which highlights team gaps and obvious opportunities for repositioning and reorganization.

The Team Map on page 207 is loosely based on my own eight-person team at The Table Group, with some names changed to protect the innocent. Note that each section includes only the names of team members who have genius or frustration in that particular area. Of course, it is easy to ascertain which of the team members has a working competency in a given area; if their name is not on the genius or frustration list, they belong in the competency category. The reason for displaying only geniuses and frustrations is to highlight those areas where a team may have a challenge.

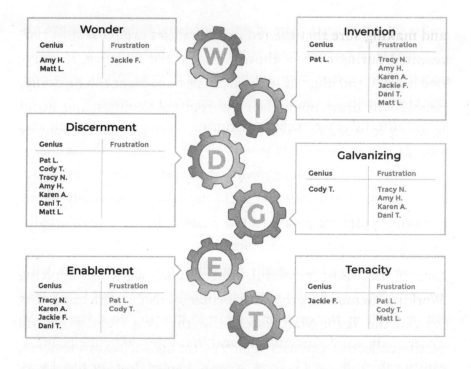

Even a cursory glance at the map for my team from a couple of years ago reveals a few clear issues.

First, notice that there is only one person on the team with the Genius of Invention. That would be me. This may or may not be a problem, depending on a number of factors, including the nature of the work we do and the amount of my time that I can dedicate to Invention. In our case, it was a problem because I was spending an inordinate amount of my time in another area, and that area was not one of my geniuses. I'll explain more about this in a moment.

Second, notice that there is only one person on the team with the Genius of Tenacity. Again, this may or may not be a problem. As it turned out, it was. More on that soon.

Next, notice that there is only one person on the team with the Genius of Galvanizing. Not only that but notice how many people have *Galvanizing* as their area of frustration, meaning that they would be unlikely to step up and galvanize.

Finally, there are other interesting things to notice on the map. A high percentage of people on the team have Discernment as a genius. We also have plenty of people who are geniuses at Enablement. That means that decision-making is generally sound given the levels of collective intuition, and that we are not usually lacking for people willing to pitch in.

Now, let's get back to the potential problems, starting with Galvanizing. The team's only galvanizer is Cody, but Cody was not in a role at that time that allowed him to galvanize. As the leader of the team, it seemed logical that I should be the primary galvanizer. And since it is an area of competency for me, I was fairly good at it. And so, I spent a lot of my time and energy Galvanizing. This was a problem for two reasons.

First, it limited the amount of time and energy I could spend doing Invention, which is something that gave me joy and energy, and which the team needed. Second, I was getting burned out by having to galvanize so much. That's what happens when we spend *too much* time doing something we're good at but that isn't an area of genius. I began to get frustrated seeing all the Invention that needed to be done—which I tried to do at night and on weekends—and I resented coming to work and finding myself constantly Galvanizing.

As it turned out, I wasn't the only one in this predicament.

Having only one team member with Tenacity was even more of an insufficiency than our lack of Invention. Within most organizations, there is a need for more people to be getting things done than there is for them to be coming up with new ideas. There is the old saying that work is 10 percent inspiration and 90 percent perspiration. I don't know if those numbers are accurate, but I do know that they are directionally correct.

One of our team members, Tracy, had Tenacity in her area of competency, and because she is also a genius at Enablement, it was easy for people to ask her to dive into Tenacity-oriented work. A lot. And she always said yes, and quite frankly, did it extremely well. For a long time. When we reviewed our Team Map, she blurted out, "That's the problem! I'm so tired of doing Tenacity work but all of it seems to land on my desk!" And we knew she was right. Moreover, Tracy wanted to exercise her Discernment more, something that is a real area of genius for her, but she was regularly putting off that work in order to finish projects and push things through to completion.

To make matters worse, among Tracy's various responsibilities, she is also my editor. That is a great role for someone with the Genius of Discernment, evaluating another person's ideas and providing insightful feedback. Well, with me sacrificing Invention in favor of Galvanizing, and Tracy pushing off Discernment to do Tenacity work, it is no surprise that we were frequently behind schedule getting books written. Just as important, though, was the fact that both Tracy and I were experiencing increasing levels of burnout.

Low-Hanging Fruit

The problems within our department were validated as soon as we saw the report. If we wanted to improve our productivity and morale—and who doesn't?—we needed to reduce the amount of time that Tracy spent in Tenacity and that I, Pat, spent Galvanizing so that we could contribute more in our areas of genius. This would be good for the company and for us as individuals. It wasn't a matter of stopping those activities altogether—Tracy and I knew that we needed to do things outside of our geniuses— it was about reducing them to a manageable level.

As a result of this clarity, the answers became so much easier to see. We decided to tap into Cody's Galvanizing skills by having him run daily meetings to keep people focused and moving forward on tactical initiatives. His level of contribution and excitement increased immediately, as did my sense of freedom and relief! Seriously. Today, we call him our Chief Galvanizing Officer.

As for Tracy, we agreed that everyone in the office who had Tenacity as an area of competency needed to share the load with her. And Tracy needed to show us all of the things she was doing that were overloading her so that we could begin taking them off her plate.

Beyond that, we had a clear understanding of the skills that our next additions to the team should have. We hired a wonderful woman who had Discernment and Tenacity as her geniuses. We even hired a great guy who had Invention and Galvanizing. It's important to make it clear that both of these people first had to be cultural fits with our company, as well as having the geniuses that we needed and often lacked.

The impact that all of this had on our productivity (aka ability to get more done in less time) and morale (aka excitement about coming to work eager and leaving with peace at the end of the day) was tangible. Without the Working Genius Team Map, we would not have been able to see the problems as clearly or address them so quickly.

Here's another example of a team report that provided clarity and quick action for a team.

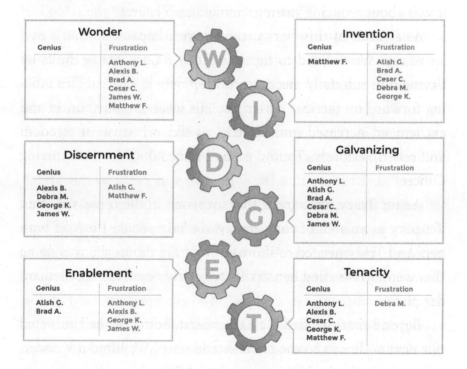

I worked with the leadership team of a large technology company that had been lagging behind its competitors for a number of years in terms of product development and innovation. Unsurprisingly, their market share, revenue, and profit margins were not where they needed to be.

They agreed to take the Working Genius Assessment, and I must admit that I think their expectations were low. Many executives are skeptical about personality assessments, and I wasn't sure how they would respond.

As you can see, none of the team members had Wonder as a Working Genius. Not only that, a big portion of the team had it as their working frustration. Beyond that, only one team member had Invention as a Working Genius, and he was their lawyer! Keep in mind that this was a technology company.

Almost immediately after seeing their report, one of the more skeptical members of the team said, "Here is our problem. We never Wonder. We don't contemplate what is going on in the market, what our customers might need, where we're headed. We're all about Tenacity and getting things done."

I couldn't believe that the statement was made so quickly after seeing the results, and I was surprised, though pleased, that the person who said it was one of the last people I would have expected. He went on. "We have to start carving out time to Wonder, and we need to stop making every meeting about agendas and numbers and to-do lists." And everyone agreed. Frankly, I couldn't believe it. They had diagnosed their issue and accepted that diagnosis much more readily than if I had pointed it out as a consultant.

In addition to committing to taking more time to Wonder, the team went a step further. Recognizing and confirming that the lawyer had Invention as a genius, they actually changed his job description to include responsibility for new technology acquisition. He was ecstatic about getting to use his genius, and the team was relieved to have someone who had that skill in charge of an area of such importance. I can tell you that there is little chance they would have made such a nontraditional move without having seen their problem so clearly displayed in their Team Map.

WORKING GENIUS AND ORGANIZATIONAL HEALTH

For the past twenty-five years, all of us at The Table Group have been working to make organizations healthier and more effective through better leadership, teamwork, clarity, communication, and human systems. We've always believed, and still do, that organizational health is even more important than organizational intelligence. By minimizing politics and confusion, leaders can improve productivity, engagement, and loyalty, which will allow them to fully tap into their strategic advantages and accomplish what dysfunctional organizations could never dream of.

Where does Working Genius fit into all that? Even though the Six Types model emerged from my own pursuit of joy and energy at work, I've since come to realize that it is absolutely central to organizational health, and in more ways than I could have imagined. Let me attempt to identify all the ways that this applies.

First, a leadership team cannot be cohesive if its members don't understand and tap into one another's geniuses. This is a topic worthy of its own book. The difference between a leadership team that adjusts its roles and work based on its members' geniuses and one that relies only on job titles and generic expectations is almost beyond description.

Second, Working Genius is central to productivity. When people in an organization understand and are transparent about their areas of genius—and frustration—leaders can make adjustments that bring about significantly greater contributions from employees. At the end of the day, people get more done, in less time, and with less friction. Measuring the impact of this is almost impossible, as it permeates nearly every aspect of an employee's experience.

Third, and related to the previous point, Working Genius is as fundamental to employee retention, engagement, and morale as any other factor. When people in an organization know that their geniuses are being utilized and appreciated by their managers, they are going to come to work with more passion and enthusiasm, and they are going to be much less likely to abandon the organization during difficult times. They are going to tell others about their experience at the company, attracting new employees and customers alike.

Finally, the most important activity in any organization is going to be transformed when the people who are participating in it know and understand their Working Geniuses and frustrations. I'm talking about meetings. When people know what kind of conversation they are having, and when they tap into their geniuses during those conversations, they make better decisions and buy into those decisions in ways that other teams cannot fathom.

I am utterly convinced that, as much as anything I've ever

done in the world of organizational development and effectiveness, Working Genius lies at the foundation of it all. When human beings are fully alive at work, whether they are the founder, the CEO, or the most recent hire, they are much more likely to contribute to an organization's health, and help it avoid the perils of dysfunction.

MY HOPE FOR WORKING GENIUS

It is painful to think that there are many people in the world who are stuck in jobs or roles that don't align with their Working Geniuses, and that force them to live within their frustrations. And it's even worse to know that many of them don't know why they are miserable. It's my hope that by reading this book and taking the Working Genius Assessment, many of those people will be able to identify and make adjustments that reduce their misery. I'm glad to say that since we launched the assessment two years ago, we've been hearing from people around the world who are doing just that. And the stories we receive go beyond people's professional lives, impacting their marriages, families, and friendships even more than we had expected.

Kristal—business owner

Kristal was on the verge of burnout and "getting ready to sell the business" when she discovered the Working Genius model. She took the assessment and within fifteen minutes made the realization that she was working almost entirely outside of her areas of Working Genius, and mostly doing the things that drained her of joy and energy. That week, she had all of her staff take the assessment, and they immediately reorganized the team so that she, and everyone else, could spend more of their time in their areas of genius. We followed up with her a month later and asked, "Are you still planning to sell?" She replied, "Not a chance; this is the most fulfilled I've been in years!"

Kevin—church pastor

Kevin sent us an email with the subject line "Wow." He explained that he had been a pastor for almost twenty years, and that he had lived under constant guilt and pressure that he wasn't good at his vocation. It was heavy. He went on to explain that he struggled to come up with creative and inspiring sermons, which drained him and left him feeling inadequate on Sunday mornings. After taking the assessment and discovering that Invention was not one of his geniuses, he felt liberated. He came to the realization that every pastor can't be gifted in all areas. Kevin admitted that he really enjoyed and was good at providing counseling and support to the people in his church, and that rather than trying to overcome his struggles with creative sermonizing, he could tap into the geniuses of other people on his team to help him in that area. His vocation was no longer in question, and his guilt and self-judgment were greatly reduced. Hallelujah!

Heath—husband

Heath wrote to us and said, "I thought my wife hated me." He was exaggerating, and partly joking, but admitted that, at times, he felt that there was some truth to it. Wow. He explained that he loved coming up with new ideas, but that he was often discouraged because he felt that his wife would usually shoot them down by criticizing them. Well, on their wedding anniversary, Heath and his wife took the Working Genius Assessment and discovered he had the Genius of Invention (new ideas) and his wife had the Genius of Discernment (evaluating those ideas). They both realized that she was not meaning to discourage him at all, but rather to provide helpful feedback and Discernment to her husband, whom she cared about deeply. She actually wanted to make sure that his ideas might be successful, and the best way to do that was to evaluate and suggest adjustments that would save her husband time, energy, and potential disappointment. Heath said that this realization helped them resolve years of subtle frustration in their relationship, and was the best anniversary present.

These stories were sent to us unprompted within the first ninety days of the assessment's launch. Since then, we have continued to receive countless similar stories from people whose jobs, careers, and lives have been almost immediately improved by making simple realizations about their God-given talents. I can say with confidence that I have never worked on anything that has had such an immediate impact on people's lives.

MORE PEACE—LESS GUILT, JUDGMENT, AND BURNOUT

At the end of the day, the reason for understanding ourselves and others is to bring about more peace, within ourselves and in our relationships with others. There is nothing soft or theoretical about this.

For so many people, one of the biggest stealers of peace is having to do work that doesn't suit their natural, God-given strengths. But because most of these people don't realize that, they end up feeling really bad about themselves (aka guilty) for not being better at what they are doing. That kind of guilt is unnecessary and leads to serious problems in the lives of workers and the people they love.

All of us can relate to this. We've felt bad about ourselves for not being good at some kind of work, and most of us have beaten ourselves up for it. I did it in my own life early in my career. "Why can't I do this as well as my colleagues? What is wrong with me?" The answer to that question should have been, "Because they're doing what they enjoy and are naturally adept at doing, and I'm not!" But because I didn't understand that, I felt guilty and attributed my struggles to lack of effort or intelligence, or worse yet, virtue.

Judgment is similar, except that it's what we do when we see a colleague struggle in some kind of work and incorrectly attribute their struggle to their lack of effort, intelligence, or virtue. "I don't know why he can't get that done. I think he just doesn't care. Or maybe he's just not as smart as we thought he was. Or is it possible that he just isn't committed to the team?" We've all done this, and it's dangerous and destructive. It causes people to feel hurt and rejected, and it adversely impacts teams, organizations, even families.

The key to avoiding inappropriate guilt and judgment is gaining a better understanding of ourselves and others. When we know our own, and one another's, strengths and weaknesses, most of that guilt and judgment will go away, replaced by empathy and productive support. We'll be able to say to ourselves, "I really am bad at this. Maybe I should find a better way to contribute, one that lines up with my skills and talents." And we'll look at others who are struggling and say, "Is that the right role for you? Maybe there is a better way to use your skills and talents."

Now, it's worth saying that some people do have a poor work ethic, or lack intelligence, or even virtue. And they need to be dealt with accordingly, though compassionately. But in so many of the cases I see, people who struggle are unaware of how their work and their gifts are misaligned. And that's what this book and this model are designed to address.

Avoiding Burnout

A different but related problem experienced by many people who are stuck doing work that is not aligned with their gifts is burnout. And while no one gets to spend all of their time doing what they love—we all have to do things in our areas of frustration from time to time—those who find themselves trapped in work that gives them no joy or energy almost never succeed, and certainly don't thrive. They get burned out.

What's interesting about this is that the *type* of work that a person does turns out to be much more important in regard to burnout than the *volume* of work. Some people can work long hours over extended periods of time in their areas of joy and passion, while others can work relatively few hours but experience severe burnout because they are doing work that robs them of joy and passion. It follows logically, then, that a person who is experiencing the first signs of burnout will not find relief simply by reducing the time they spend at work, even though that is often what we prescribe for them. What they need to do is spend more time doing what feeds them.

Whether it's guilt, judgment, or burnout that is causing someone to lose their peace in the course of work, I am excited to know that the Working Genius model can help them turn things around. And that matters. Because I believe God gives people gifts so they can use them to do good, and I hope the insights they get from this book will allow them to do just that.

Acknowledgments

There are many people to thank for helping me with this book, especially given all of the people who took part in the early development of the Working Genius model.

Thanks to Tracy, Amy, and Kim, who were in the room when it all came about, and to Amy for asking the Wonder question that prompted this invention. And to Tracy, Karen, Cody, and Matt for the hours of feedback and editing and Discernment. Your countless ideas and suggestions are impossible to acknowledge, or even remember, but I am grateful for your intelligence and passion.

Thanks to my wife, Laura, and all our boys for living with a whiteboard in our family room for a few months as we developed the model early on. And to Laura for being so passionate about it all, and for the idea of turning the model into interconnected gears. I loved applying the model with all of you and your friends.

Thanks to all the unsuspecting victims who wandered into our home and office and were forced to take the assessment in the early days. Your openness and enthusiasm were more important than you know.

Thanks to everyone at The Table Group for your contribution and enthusiasm around the assessment, the podcast, the certification program, and the book. And to all of our consultants around the world who have embraced and shared the Working Genius with clients. Your passion and energy around this are so inspiring to us. And to the Amazing Parish team who were the first organization to embrace the model and use it with passion.

Thanks to Matt Holt and the BenBella team for your patience, flexibility, and commitment to this book.

And, of course, I give genuine thanks to God, for every part of life itself, and for allowing me and our team to play a role in helping You help people understand the gifts that You have given them to contribute to a better world for themselves and the people they serve.

About the Author

Patrick Lencioni is founder and president of The Table Group, a firm dedicated to protecting human dignity in the world of work, personal development, and faith. For the past twenty-five years, Pat and his team have been providing organizations with ideas, products, and services that improve teamwork, clarity, and employee engagement. He is also the cofounder of The Amazing Parish organization.

Lencioni's passion for organizations and teams is reflected in his writing, speaking, executive consulting, and most recently his three podcasts, *At the Table with Patrick Lencioni, The Working Genius Podcast,* and *The Simple Reminder.*

Pat is the author of twelve best-selling books with over seven million copies sold. His capstone book, *The Advantage*, is the preeminent and original source on organizational health. After twenty years in print, his classic book *The Five Dysfunctions of a Team* remains a weekly fixture on national best-seller lists.

As one of the most sought-after speakers and consultants in the world, Pat has been able to work with and address a wide variety of organizations including Fortune 100 companies, small- to medium-sized enterprises, start-ups, professional sports teams, schools, and churches. He has been featured in numerous publications, including the *Wall Street Journal*, *Harvard Business Review*, *USA Today*, *Inc.* magazine, and *Chief Executive* magazine.

Pat has been married to his wife, Laura, for thirty years, and they have four wonderful sons.